*Alexia Amvrazi, Diana Farr Louis
and Diane Shugart*

# 111 Places
# in Athens
# That You
# Shouldn't Miss

*Photographs by Yannis Varouhakis*

T0350612

emons:

© Emons Verlag GmbH
All rights reserved
Photographs by Yannis Varouhakis
© Cover motif: shutterstock.com/dnd_project
Layout: Eva Kraskes, based on a design
by Lübbeke | Naumann | Thoben
Edited by Rosalind Horton
Maps: altancicek.design, www.altancicek.de
Basic cartographical information from Openstreetmap,
© OpenStreetMap-Mitwirkende, ODbL
Printing and binding: CPI – Clausen & Bosse, Leck
Printed in Germany 2018 (II)
ISBN 978-3-7408-0377-3
First edition

Did you enjoy it? Do you want more?
Join us in uncovering new places around the world on:
www.111places.com

# Foreword

First-time visitors to Athens are often shocked by how modern it is. The timeless buildings of the Acropolis seemingly hover over a swirl of ephemera. Compressed between a glorious past and the ever-changing present are layers of the city's Classical, Roman, Byzantine and Ottoman periods, tamped down by a fairly short modern history that comprises wars, occupations, dictatorships, renewed democracy and their aftermaths.

The best way to let the city get under your skin is to have no pre-conceptions and experience it with an open heart. Although it's a sprawling megalopolis, its most interesting quarters are easy to get to and brimming with contrasts. The unending economic 'crisis' has hit some areas hard, but the challenges have also inspired startling creativity, higher service standards and divergent trends. The places we've chosen to present here range from the ancient to the ultramodern and reflect a city that's impossible to categorise. They reflect its protean capacity to surprise and inspire, its addictive spontaneity, a liberating energy and candidly bright light.

We have tried to bring you to people and places that reveal the many layers, not always immediately visible, of a complex city. Passionately lively Athens is never boring, frequently quirky and tongue-in-cheek in its approach to life, sometimes darkly disturbing, and always intriguing.

Like most of its residents, we came to Athens by different paths, but what we share is a deep and unshakable love for the city. Its greatest appeal is what drove us to write this book – the ceaseless pleasure of discovering new places and facets even at the most visited spots. With a spirit of adventure, humour, respect and the often challenging dilemma of having to select 111 rather than 1,111 places to share with you, we savoured our explorations and hope that you will too, every step of the way.

*Alexia Amvrazi, Diana Farr Louis and Diane Shugart*

# 111 Places

# 1 1900 The Barber Shop

*Grooming in a totally retro 'decompression room'*

Meandering the side streets of Monastiraki or Psyrri you may notice a few nondescript barber shops straight out of the 1950s, while in trendier areas like Koukaki or Kolonaki you'll spot barber shops with vintage touches and tattooed hairstylists. But 1900 The Barber Shop is an entirely different story. It was envisaged by a Greek with refined old-school tastes and a strikingly dapper style, whose family lived in Cairo for four generations. Growing up in elegant surroundings adorned by antiques and culture, in his own home, as well as those of French, British and American friends, created in him an aesthetic world that he has translated in this shop.

Panayiotis Grigoriou is an entrepreneur who worked for 20 years in marketing management for major companies, but since the '90s he began to visualise opening his own barber shop. He sought to stand out commercially and offer men treatment fit for gentlemen – indeed most of his clientele are businessmen, politicians, actors and diplomats. His greatest goal was to recreate his fond personal memories from the barber shops in Cairo during his childhood. 'My dad took me to the barber shop, where I experienced a sense of male bonding; vibrant conversations and a relaxing sense of being pampered.'

Advertised as a 'gentlemen's club' of sorts, 1900 is what he describes as a stylish, yet accessibly priced, 'decompression room'. Wooden floors, plush sofas, books, a drinks tray, chandeliers, vintage artworks and quirky details like a magnum champagne lamp are the *mise-en-scène* for this no-woman's land. Most of the décor is from 1880 to 1920, with an ambience one would feel in an old villa that's comfortably worn around the edges. Apart from classic-style hair cutting, grooming inspired from Cairo includes face massage, hot towels and a deep shave, lighters to burn away ear hairs, manicures, pedicures and threading.

Address Ipsilantou 35 & Ploutarchou, Kolonaki, Athens 10676, +30 210 7220511 | Getting there Metro to Evangelismos (M3) | Hours Mon, Wed & Sat 10am–3pm; Tue, Thu & Fri 10.30am–8.30pm | Tip Just south of Evangelismos metro station, explore the lush archaeological site of Aristotle's Lyceum, the gymnasia where the Peripatetic School was born.

# 2 — Agia Marina

*A church resting on a pre-Christian grotto*

On the Hill of Nymphs, near the National Observatory of Athens, stands a large, cream-coloured church dedicated to Saint Marina, a young woman who is also known as the Vanquisher of Demons.

Imposing in appearance, with domed tiled roofs and marble steps that sparkle in the sunlight, the church was built between 1924 and 1927 in the Byzantine style. The four-aisled basilica stands in memory of a 15-year-old maiden of incredible beauty who suffered inconceivable torture and disfigurement at the hands of a man who wanted her as his bride. She told him he could never have her because the only man she had love for was Christ and challenged him to torture her in any way he wished to test her devotion, and so he did, in a multitude of gruesome ways. He even sent a demon to devour her in her prison cell, but she demolished it – using a hammer.

The church is imposing but unremarkable, unlike its history. It was actually built on the grounds of a much smaller, post-Byzantine church dedicated to the same saint; the elaborately carved main altar and several icons came from that original church. And then there's the most intriguing surprise of all – an ancient grotto with a domed roof through which natural light streams, nestled in the south eastern corner of the church. With an intensely tranquil and mystical ambience ideally suited to sacred liturgies, the 'cave' dates back to the pre-Christian era when it was used as a place of worship. Centuries later it functioned as an aqueduct, while in the present day it is used for baptisms. Interestingly, Marina is also the saint of pregnant women and children.

Archaeological excavations in the cave during the 1980s unearthed seven layers of walls from the 13th, 17th, 18th and 19th centuries, and frescoes from those walls are exhibited, together with other religious relics, in the northern part of the present-day church.

Address Agias Marinas 1, Thissio, Athens 11851 | Getting there Metro to Thissio (M 1) | Hours Daily 10am – 1pm | Tip Return to the present and blend into the neighbourhood's vibrant café culture by bagging a perfect people-watching post at Athinaion Politia café-restaurant.

# 3 Agioi Isidoroi

*Church cover for a rebel's escape route?*

Agioi Isidoroi, which sits against the western slope of Lycabettus Hill, is one of those ordinary churches found throughout Athens and, indeed, Greece – neither especially pretty nor particularly well-known. One apparent oddity is its name, which uses the plural form of saint, although there was just one Saint Isidore to whom the church is dedicated. But on closer inspection, something else stands out: the church isn't simply built against the grey rock, but into it.

The church was built in the 15th or 16th century by a monk on the spot where Agios Isidoros – a Greek commander in the Roman army who was martyred for preaching Christianity – came to him in a dream. The interior is as plain as its flat, white-washed exterior, except for a gold-edged icon screen and a few icons hung on the rock walls. But the church's true purpose may have not been as a place of worship, but to conceal the opening of a tunnel linking Lycabettus to Galatsi, part of an escape route to the Penteli mountains that was used by Greek revolutionaries during the Greek War of Independence. This would not be uncommon, as numerous churches throughout Greece are said to have been built on particular sites for similar purposes. Whether the passage, if it existed, was also used by resistance fighters during World War II is not known.

A sign inside the church confirms the underground passage (while also mentioning that the church is the area's oldest and was celebrated for its many miracles). But the possibility of a tunnel's existence is not far-fetched. The supposed entrance is behind a glass screen but seems wide enough for someone to squeeze through. Lycabettus is part of the Tourkovounia ridge where Galatsi sits. While the city has grown to a point where it is hard to imagine such a link, the opening in the rock may have been formed millennia ago by water coursing down the slopes.

Address Sarantapihou 61, Lycabettus, Athens 10210, + 30 210 3633282 | Getting there Bus 60 or X54 | Hours Daily 8am – noon | Tip Follow the sign to the cave of Agios Aristidis, a disciple of Saint Paul who took refuge here from the Romans. To enter, you'll need to ask the verger for the keys.

# 4  Agios Nikolaos Ragavas

*The bell tolls only for freedom*

On 12 October, 1944, residents of the Plaka district woke up to an unusual sound: the pealing of the bell of Agios Nikolaos Ragavas. It was a startling sound as unlike the other churches in this old quarter, and throughout the city, this bell rings only on special occasions. This was just such an occasion: the city's liberation from the Germans.

Built on the north-eastern foothill of the Acropolis rock facing the city's other hill, Lycabettus, Agios Nikolaos Ragavas was the private chapel of the Ragavas family, a prominent Byzantine clan that counts the Emperor Michael Rangabe among its members. But this association has faded into the history of the 11th-century church, which is focused on its famous bell – not the bell hanging in the free-standing domed tower but the one carefully guarded inside the church.

During the 400 years of Ottoman rule, the ringing of church bells was forbidden. Accordingly, the Turkish authorities removed or destroyed all the bells. These were gradually restored after independence, but Agios Nikolaos Ragavas was the first to receive one – perhaps because of the church founders' noble connections. (By one account, the priests had hidden the bell before it could be destroyed.) In 1834, when Athens was established as the capital of modern Greece and King Otto arrived to take his throne, it was the only church bell in the city to ring in his arrival.

The bell, a gift from Russia, which had supported the Greek independence cause, was commissioned in Italy. It is decorated with reliefs depicting the crucifixion, the Apostle Paul and the Virgin Mary and, according to a Latin inscription, is 'the work of Alexander and brother'. Nowadays the bell is only rung on 25 March, the annual commemoration of the start of the Greek independence revolt. Locals quip that they hope not to hear its peal on any other day as that is likely to mean bad luck.

Address Prytaneiou 1, Plaka, Athens 10558, +30 210 3228193 | Getting there Metro to Monastiraki (M1 & M3) | Tip Ayios Ioannis Theologos (Erechtheos and Erotokritou) preserves frescoes from the 11th to 13th centuries. Morosini based two cannons here during his siege of the Acropolis in 1687.

# 5 — Agios Nikolaos Thon

*The city's modern history in a small round church*

The intersection of Alexandras and Kifissias avenues is one of the city's busiest, the hub of traffic between the centre of Athens and its northern suburbs. Thousands of people whiz past every day, with barely a sideways glance at an architectural oddity just 20 metres from the kerb: the 19th-century Agios Nikolaos Thon. But this little church is worth noting for more than the curiosity of its round shape: layered into its masonry are important moments in the history of modern Athens.

Like many of the city's surviving neoclassical gems, the church was designed by the architect Ernst Ziller as a chapel on the sprawling estate of Nikolaos Thon – who rather immodestly named it after himself and decorated it with a diamond cross and solid gold church vessels.

A member of the court of George I, the Danish prince chosen to replace the unpopular Otto as king, Thon was a wealthy businessman and landowner who was also involved in organising the 1906 Olympic Games. Shortly afterwards, he passed away and in 1921, his family sold the estate to two developers who sold or leased different sections as a clinic, school, beer garden, barracks and prison. But the mansion and church remained until the former was firebombed in the 1944 'Dekemvriana' clashes that marked the start of the Greek civil war. Decades later, the church found itself at the heart of a heated development battle over this prime piece of property. Locals seeking to preserve the small family-run businesses fought a fierce battle but lost out to developers, who were nonetheless forced to erect their high-rise office complex around the church.

Today the church is encased in scaffolding as part of a slow restoration process but it's easy to peep through for a glimpse of the once-lavish interior with its pretty frescoes and gospel, open on the stand, as if services are about to commence.

Address Corner of Leoforos Kifissias and Leoforos Alexandras, Ampelokipi, Athens 11523 | Getting there Metro to Ampelokipi (M 3); bus 3, 10, 14, 18, 19, 230, 550, A 5 or A 7 | Hours Accessible from the outside only | Tip Check out the hand-painted movie posters advertising the latest shows at the Athinaion cinema about a block south – a real treat for cinephiles!

# 6 Agios Sostis

*A church designed for a World's Fair in Paris*

Wanting to change its image from the eternal association with antiquity, Greece assigned a French architect to design a Byzantine church using the most revolutionary construction materials of the time as its pavilion for the 1900 World's Fair in Paris. Though it followed the traditional form with a dome and a brick façade, the frame was wrought iron, the dome was supported by cast-iron pillars and arches with plant motifs, and the bricks were larger than usual, glazed salmon pink, interspersed with turquoise ceramic bands.

But its purpose was commercial, not religious, a showcase for Greek products like tobacco, wines, textiles and copies of ancient statues, as well as contemporary Greek painters.

The Fair was the largest ever, coinciding with the second Modern Olympics, but failed to turn a profit. It did leave some memorable buildings – the Grand Palais and Petit Palais, the Quai d'Orsay (now Musée d'Orsay) and the gilded Pont Alexandre III – while the Eiffel Tower was painted yellow for the occasion.

Two years before, an attempt had been made on the life of the Greek king, George I, and when the fair was over, the Mayor of Athens, Spyros Mercouris, grandfather of *Never on Sunday*'s Melina, had the church dismantled, brought to the city, and erected on the spot of the failed assassination. It was dedicated in 1903 to the Holy Saviour in thanks for miraculously sparing the king.

Alas, his luck did not hold and in 1913, King George was murdered in Thessaloniki six months before his golden jubilee. He was the longest reigning Greek monarch and grandfather of the Duke of Edinburgh.

Surrounded by tall cypresses, the church stands out like a jewel among the glass office buildings and hotels on Syngrou Avenue, while everything in the interior is worth a close look, especially the intricately carved woodwork, the unusual columns and the fine frescoes.

**Address** Syngrou 133, Neos Kosmos, Athens 11745, +30 210 9335460, www.sostis.gr | **Getting there** Bus 040, 106, 126, 136, 550, A 2, B 2 or trolley 10 | **Hours** Daily 7am–6pm (matins at 7am and evensong at 5pm) | **Tip** The broad avenue linking the sea and central Athens was created at the same time as the church. It is named after Andreas Syngros, a Greek banker/philanthropist from Istanbul, who funded it along with the Corinth Canal, hospitals, and many other good works.

# 7 __ Al Hammam
*Steamy treatments, Turkish-style*

Stepping off the buzzy Plaka tourist trail onto more tranquil Tripodon Street you'll arrive at an old Greek house-turned-bathhouse. Decorated with brightly coloured, traditional Turkish ornamental tiles and wall designs, stained-glass fittings and carved wooden sofas, it offers the authentic relaxing hammam experience in a more urban, modern and slightly Europeanised rendition.

This is the second hammam created by its owner Nikos Marinakis, the first being in Chania, Crete, where he was inspired by Minoan bath chambers unearthed at Knossos, as well as the centuries-old hammam culture of the island's Turkish population. Upon discovering Athens' Bathhouse of the Winds on Kyrrestou Street in Plaka, built during the first Ottoman occupation (1458 – 1669), and used until 1956 (today it is a visitable museum), he created Al Hammam in a derelict building just 100 metres away.

The tradition of using hot water and steam for physical detoxification began in the Neolithic age, and in Greece bathing rituals date as far back as 2400 B.C. (the Bronze Age) while bathing facilities became popular in Greek cities from the 6th century B.C., usually built near gymnasiums for post-workout cleansing. It was the Romans who made bathing rituals more sophisticated, building bathhouses (named 'balnae' from the Greek 'balaneion' for 'bath') that also became hot social hubs. The Turks adopted and reinvented the ritual after the 7th century. Designed to purify both body and soul, the hammam experience begins with sweating it out in a circular marble steam room. After half an hour, you can lie on a marble bed and get lathered up with sudsy black olive oil soap. This is followed by a hair wash / head massage and vigorous body scrub. The ending is somewhat shocking as cold water is poured over you to raise the blood pressure and reawaken the senses, effectively returning you to reality.

**Address** 16 Tripodon & Ragava 10, Plaka, Athens 10558, +30 211 0129099, www.alhammam.gr | **Getting there** Metro to Monastiraki (M1 & M3) | **Hours** Daily 11am–10pm | **Tip** On the same street, you'll find the unique School Life and Education Museum, which is like a visual postcard depicting the country's education system and traditions from 1700 to today.

# 8 __ Albandakis' Stone Stories

*A cave for geologists, healers and gem-lovers*

The only tourists you'll see here are bright-eyed seekers travelling the world and stopping over to find the perfect crystal to place into a pouch. Bang in the heart of Athens on noisy, narrow Perikleous Street, this somewhat mystical shop instantly shifts you into a floaty state, as everywhere you look there are glittering crystals, oddly coloured minerals and rough fossils, each radiating its own energy.

Designed to create the feeling of a cave with hollows (in the depth of the shop there is even the fossilised skeleton of the 15,000-year-old *Ursus uralensis*), the store presents naturally formed stones and minerals on the left side and shaped, polished crystals on the right.

Angels, ovals and even phalluses, as well as a wide selection of pendulums, catch the eye. In the central area are rows of boxes overflowing with healing crystals, from deep blue lapis lazuli and mercurial black hematite to soft pink rose quartz. Each box is labelled with the stone's name and healing qualities, and the expected ritual is to move along them and sense which stone calls to you. The knowledgeable staff are happy to tell you more; otherwise there's usually the opportunity to ask one of the healers shopping here, often found chatting in a Hogwarts School ambience.

Opened in 1985, the store was the brainchild of geologist Nicholas Albandakis, who first discovered Prase, a rare, green quartz, on Serifos island. Originally the shop catered chiefly to geologists and jewellers, but in the early 90s they began to exhibit healing stones as New Age interest blossomed in Athens. By 2005, the healing stones became the star products. Now there are thousands to choose from, as well as CDs, aura and room sprays, books, and instruments such as crystal singing bowls. At the same time, geologists can still feel at home here, as specialised drilling equipment, tools and books are sold too.

Address Perikleous 44, Athens 10562, +30 210 3231661 | Getting there Metro to Syntagma (M2 & M3) | Hours Mon–Fri 9am–5pm, Sat 10am–3pm | Tip Did you find a crystal that whetted your appetite? Head to Just Made, round the corner on Evangelistrias 33, for fresh, inventive food on the hoof.

# 9   The Altar of Freedom
*Kaisariani memorial to resistance fighters*

To look head on at your death is unnerving. There is no way to describe what someone might feel at that moment, but the memorial at the Kaisariani shooting range to the 200 resistance fighters executed by the Nazis on 1 May, 1944, somehow manages to convey that horror. And that dignity. The memorial was installed in 2005: a 'corridor' of a dozen slabs of black granite in front of two shallow pools and a stepped walk that ends at two seven-metre- high rectangular columns in front of the old wall. Inscribed on the black granite are the names of all 739 people executed here by the Nazis. This is the Altar of Freedom, designed by sculptor Apostolos Fanakidis. But it's that old cement wall and the machine gun laid on the ground on the other side that hold the eye. It's the execution site of the 200 Greek People's Liberation Army (ELAS) fighters in reprisal for the death of a German general in an ambush near Sparta three days earlier, on 27 April.

Kaisariani, settled initially by refugees from the 1922 Asia Minor Catastrophe, is a constant in a city as variable as Athens. Its surface has changed – there are modern cafés, retail franchises, bars – but it retains a strong association with the Communist Party. This dates back to the resistance and the civil war that followed; fighting during both is detailed in a local newspaper published very briefly in 1945. The only surviving copies of two issues of *Kaisariani* are held in an exhibition area by the monument. Housed in a renovated 1910 building, the displays offer context for both Kaisariani and the Altar of Freedom – a mix of documents, clippings, discarded weapons and personal items like the rug on which resistance leader Aris Velouhiotis slept.

Ironically, access to the Altar of Freedom is no longer open because of repeated acts of vandalism. But the museum attendants will happily unlock its gate for visitors.

Address Skopeftirio, Athens 16121, +30 210 7647751 | Getting there Bus 224 or 732 |
Hours Mon & Wed 5–9pm, Tue & Fri 9am–2pm, Sat 10am–1pm | Tip Ai Yiannis
Park, a 15-minute walk away, is a perfect picnic spot with wooden swings and jungle
gym for kids and a nearby café.

# 10 The Apivita Experience
*Life as inspired by ancient medicine and bees*

Although Athenians are by now well into cosmetics by international brands, the age-old spirit of honouring holistic wisdom inspired by legendary botanists such as Dioscorides and Hippocrates (whose recipes later became widely practised by country folk) remains very much alive. Perhaps this is why the Apivita Experience Store, which bases itself on Greek holistic philosophy and presents its products in a polished, Hygge-style décor is so successful. The five-floor flagship store is not unknown to locals, although what it offers beyond its feel-good cosmetics is somewhat surprising. Upon entering you'll be impressed by a giant, realistic copper olive tree that represents wisdom (as one of the symbols of the goddess Athena), nature's bounty, a communal gathering spot and healing, because of the 'liquid gold' oil it produces.

Apivita's origins go back to 1979 when pharmacist Nikos Koutsianas, also a beekeeper, began to examine the health benefits of bee products, making the first propolis soap, and later other bee products. His hearty holistic approach was unusual for that era, but his outlook proved contagious.

The flagship store in Kolonaki offers visitors a multi-level experience, starting with sinks where you can wash your hands to try the fragrant products and sip a Greek herbal tea. On the first floor are the store's juice bar and a pharmacy where you can create your own product using honey, propolis, royal jelly, pure essential oils and more with advice from an experienced chemist. The second floor houses the Apivita Academy, where botany and aromatherapy courses are run. The third floor and up are dedicated to pampering – with a 'green' hairdresser's that uses only 100 per cent natural dyes, while the fourth and fifth floors are where the Queen Bee Spa offers everything from facials to deep-tissue massage in a soothing setting with lovely views.

**Address** Solonos 6, Kolonaki, Athens 10673, +30 210 3640560, www.apivita.com |
**Getting there** Metro to Syntagma (M2 & M3) or bus 022 or 060 to Kanari | **Hours**
Mon, Wed & Sat 10am–5pm; Tue, Thu & Fri 10am–9pm | **Tip** Nearby is the Theo-
charakis Foundation where you can enjoy a coffee and snack in style at the first-floor
Merlin Café, explore the Art Shop and see an exhibition.

# 11 Ariana

*A crash course in Greek olives*

For almost a century this warehouse-like shop has sold almost nothing but olives. Open to the street, with no doors to put you off, it invites you to inspect the contents of 23 large free-standing barrels as well as smaller containers poised on shelves along the side walls. And taste them.

Perhaps you thought there were only two kinds of olives, green and black, pitted or stuffed with pimento, garlic or almond? This collection features the fruit of some 20 varieties, with emphasis on the big oval greeny ones from Amphissa, the famous olive grove below Delphi. The Kalothanasis brothers, Andreas and Mihalis, represent the third generation in this business started by their grandfather, Andreas, who came from the area, and where the olives are still processed. As Mihalis, who runs the shop, says, 'Amphissa olives grown anywhere else don't taste the same. The land, soil, climate make a difference. We deal with olives from all over Greece – tear-shaped Kalamata, tiny Cretan, wrinkly (salt-cured) *throumbes* from Thasos – and my brother knows the secrets of curing, preserving and storing them until the next season. Ideally, we'd like to run out the day the new olives arrive, and sometimes that has happened.'

The most popular and priciest are big green olives from Mount Athos, followed by blond *throumbes* from Chios. And some firm Amphissa ones are rated by size: jumbo, colossal and mammoth.

The name Ariana comes from two ancient Greek words, *ari* and *a(g)no*. It means 'very pure', like the olive tree, Athena's gift, which earned her the patronage of the city over Poseidon's salt spring in the mythical contest on the Acropolis.

But if olives are not your thing, you can feast your eyes and taste buds on a wide assortment of pickles and two kinds of capers. Those imported from Turkey are the only non-Greek item in the shop. No comparison with those from Syros, of course.

**Address** Theatrou 3, Athens 10552, +30 210 3211839 | **Getting there** Metro to Monastiraki (M1 & M3) or Omonia (M1 & M2), and a 10-minute walk | **Hours** Mon–Sat 7.30am–3.30pm | **Tip** In the heart of Athens' food and market district, there are many other shops selling just one thing, from ropes to shoelaces, eggs, flour and phyllo.

# 12 Aristotle's Lyceum
*Take a walk on the wise side*

It's a truism that if you dig in Athens, you'll strike some ancient site, although no one expected construction for a modern art museum would unearth Aristotle's famed Lyceum. The fact that this was less than five feet under makes you wonder what other marvels lurk below the city's surface.

The ancient Greek philosopher took a perambulatory approach to learning, something that the layout makes clear as you stroll the paths between the ruins of the palaestra, baths and reading room. Oddly, for a site bordered by one of the centre's busiest thorough-fares, it's both strangely quiet and wonderfully fragrant with the wild herbs – rosemary, lavender, thyme – planted around a perimeter shaded by pomegranate and other fruit trees that recreate the feeling of the sacred grove in the ancient city's suburbs where the school was located.

School in 335 B.C. Greece incorporated music and wrestling into youths' basic education. Much time was spent outdoors, with lessons often held while walking, as Aristotle believed this was when he did his best thinking. What's remarkable are the baths. At first, these were simple stalls where youths could rinse the oil and dust from their bodies. Later, they were turned into steam rooms linked by 'pipes' under the floor to the hearth in the antechamber. The heat was collected in the clay discs laid as a floor or stacked in the room. Like many spa regimens today, the steam room was followed by a cold plunge in the cistern – a remarkably simple and ingenious system that's preserved at the site.

Even a thorough tour takes less than an hour, but you'll want to linger. Tiered wooden stands at the low elevation overlooking the site are a perfect spot to rest, read a book or just take a break from the city's bustle. Don't be surprised if you can't sit for too long: there's something about this place that gets you strolling.

**Address** Rigillis 11 and Vasilissis Sofias, Athens 10675 | **Getting there** Metro to Evangelismos (M 3); bus 3, 7, 8, 13, 22, 54, 60, 100, 203, 204, 220, 221, 224, 235, 250, 608, 622, 732, 815 or A 5 | **Hours** Daily, summer 8am–8pm, winter 8am–3pm | **Tip** Continue your stroll in the adjacent gardens of Villa Ilisia, the former mansion of the Duchess of Plaisance that now houses the Byzantine Museum.

# 13 The Art Foundation

*A home for the old and the new*

Athens today has sometimes been described as 'the new Berlin', as the crisis-hit city keeps regenerating in innovative and stimulating ways, drawing artists from around the world. The need for contemporary creative expression is running deep and the formation of communities is on the rise. When The Art Foundation (T.A.F. Metamatic) set up shop in a derelict housing area in 2009, this wave had just begun. Its founders simply wanted to offer new artists the opportunity to showcase their work. At the same time, they opened a café to entice the public into visiting a fascinating space, where they were likely to end up exploring fresh, contemporary art too. Since then it has hosted 130 projects that involved 1,700 artists (without ever charging an entrance fee).

If you chanced upon its old wooden door on narrow Normanou Street, you would never imagine that behind it stands a covered up (by a canvas roof that lets in natural light) patch of 19th-century Athens. Here you'll find two crumbling buildings from 1870 to the early 1900s – a two-storey and a ground-level house, where families lived in the 10 small rooms that T.A.F. today uses for exhibition spaces. Coming from rural areas during the 1950s and accustomed to cramped quarters, several families lived there sharing a common yard; over the years, relatives have visited to see their ancestors' former homes. Today the central yard area holds a cosy, modern yet rustic café / bar with three old trees.

T.A.F. has left the houses in their original state, which makes for a stirring juxtaposition between dilapidated building features and multifaceted displays of visual, performance, photographic, installation and other art presented there, although a polished, modern gallery space was created upstairs. A shop themed on Greek souvenirs with an imaginative, artisanal style has also been set up in the space.

**Address** Normanou 5, Monastiraki, Athens 10555, +30 210 3238757, www.theartfoundation.metamatic.gr | **Getting there** Metro to Monastiraki (M 1 & M 3) | **Hours** Mon – Sat noon – 9pm, Sun noon – 7pm | **Tip** For a buzzy drink and finger food with one of the city's best views of the Acropolis, head no further than next door to Couleur Locale.

# 14 Avli Taverna
*Possibly the best meatballs in Athens*

With its slender metal door masked by graffiti and its name barely visible on the pistachio green rectangle above it, this hole-in-the-wall eatery looks like it doesn't want to be found. And yet, when you walk through it into this former courtyard – or *avli* – the welcome will be warm.

Takis, the owner, started as the delivery boy in the 1980s when this was just a coffee joint that catered to the shopkeepers in the area. Even the blue doors and shuttered windows lining this narrow courtyard led to workshops which turned out belts, plastic tablecloths and shoe leather in the days when Psyrri had more 'red lights' and tiny factories than trendy cafés, tavernas and galleries.

When his boss died and the shops gradually shut, Takis slowly expanded the menu to include food, starting with sausages and chips, but continued to fry and simmer in the alley until a few years ago when he installed a three-burner stove in the mini kitchen / pantry. He loves to cook but now leaves that to his assistants whom he's taught to make extremely tasty traditional dishes, from omelettes with pastourma to cabbage rolls to just about the best *keftedes*, Greek meatballs, we've ever gobbled. Crispy on the outside, minty and tender on the inside, they're incredibly moreish.

But Avli's fans also relish the eccentric atmosphere, the faded clippings and adverts on the walls, the mismatched plastic 'cloths' on the round tables, the old-fashioned café chairs and the plump cats sitting on them, the garlic / chilli pepper braid dangling from a drainpipe, as well as the vintage pop music purring from the radio, not to mention the prices. The only time it's likely to be empty is right after it opens. Then it slowly fills up with duos or groups of friends, Greeks and foreign residents – and friendly chatter fills the courtyard until after midnight. Takis' affection for the place is catching.

**Address** Agiou Dimitriou 12, Psyrri, Athens 10554, +30 210 3217642 | **Getting there** Metro to Monastiraki (M1 & M3) | **Hours** Daily 1pm on | **Tip** The exotic spice souk of Evripidou Street is just one short block away.

# 15 The Battleship Averof

*Lucky Uncle George's charmed life in war and peace*

When this ship is launched at Livorno in 1910, her ownership is in doubt. The Italian navy no longer needs her, and Brazil, Turkey and Greece, which covet her can't pay the bill. Enter George Averof, the philanthropist who funded the stadium for the 1896 Olympics, from beyond the grave. His will provides for a ship for the Hellenic Navy and his executors agree to cover one-third of the cost. Newly christened, she sails for London and the coronation of George V, hoping to buy ammunition there. But Britain, aware of tensions in the Aegean, refuses to sell cordite and shells.

In October 1912, the First Balkan War breaks out and, still lacking ammo, the *Averof* leaves Faliro for the Dardanelles, leading the Greek fleet. Reaching Limnos, she finally loads the vital ammunition, smuggled from England just in time.

Without one day of gunnery practice, the *Averof* engages the Ottoman fleet in two battles and defeats it handily. Hitting the enemy with deadly accuracy, while remaining unscathed, earns her the nickname 'Lucky Uncle George'. And helps Greece double its territory.

By 1941, the coal-fired ship is obsolete but her crew refuse to sink her or leave her to the Nazis and sail for Egypt and eventually to Bombay, the first Greek naval ship since Alexander's day. From 1951 to 1983, she is retired to Poros before being designated a museum. The restoration work after long neglect proves herculean, but today she gleams spotless and beloved.

Try to imagine her with 600 crew, sleeping in hammocks stored on the ceilings; and peep through the windows into the luxurious officers' quarters. Think of the heat from coal furnaces and the noise of the huge engines or when the guns fired.

Afterwards, visit the Trireme *Olympias* and the three-master *Eugenios Eugenides* (originally the *Sunbeam II* built in 1929 for British shipowner Walter Runciman, grandfather of historian Steven).

Address Greek Maritime Tradition Park, Flisvos, Palio Faliro 17561, +30 210 9888211, www.averof.mil.gr | **Getting there** Metro to Neos Kosmos (M 2) and tram; metro to Syngrou-Fix (M 2) and bus B 2 or 550; bus 101, 217, A 1 or B 1 | **Hours** Tue–Fri 9am–2pm, Sat, Sun & holidays 10am–5pm (guided tours available) | **Tip** After a look at the other ships in the park, make your way to the taverna at the marina next door for a seaside lunch.

# 16 Benaki Toy Museum

*A tower of toys and rooms full of history*

Entering the building, the museum is an experience in itself; the former 19th-century villa, designed in an eclectic, Gothic and medieval architectural style and crowned by two octagonal towers, stands out like a fairy-tale castle among jaded, sea-facing apartment blocks. Its interiors are embellished with baroque and art nouveau features on ceilings, floor tiles and walls, while its many rooms are filled with a colourful plethora of toys. The collection of 20,000 objects was donated by Maria Argyriadi, whose love for toys in childhood was reignited when she found and rescued a teddy bear as an adult. Having a peripatetic antiquarian husband facilitated her mission as she gathered and restored toys from around Europe, Africa and Asia before turning her focus to Greece.

The exhibition begins with sculpted clay and wooden dolls, horses and figurines from ancient Greece, Egypt and Rome, followed by the Byzantine era and then entering the 17th to 20th centuries. Fashionably dressed porcelain dolls with piercing eyes in fine silk and lace dresses, artful board games, mechanical monkeys, a peep show, and magnificently crafted miniature theatres are among them. Puppets are honoured too – the classical Greek Fasoulis and the 'cast' of Nikos Akiloglou's 'Puppet Theatre of Resistance', performed in the mountains during World War II – are showcased alongside Britain's Punch and Judy. For the most part, the toys here are not separated by national origin; thus the culturally inspired craftsmanship and socio-political elements of toys from different countries becomes more evident in toys from the same period.

Naturally, there is no plastic in sight – all of the toys are made of natural materials. Also noteworthy is that in bygone eras toys were either much more intricate, artful and delicate or plain and unsophisticated – but either way, always lovable to kids. There is also a wonderful gift shop with a plethora of classic and modern toys for all ages.

Address Poseidonos 14 & Tritonos Street 1, Palaio Faliro 17561, +30 212 6875280, www.benaki.gr | Getting there Bus 217, 550, 860, A 1, B 1 or B 2; tram to Trokantero | Hours Thu–Sun 10am–6pm | Tip From the museum you can see and smell the sea. Cross over to Floisvos Park, considered one of Attica's best playgrounds but also great for a seaside stroll or snacks.

# 17 Benizelos Mansion

*The last bastion of Byzantine Athens*

Newly opened to the public, the Byzantine mansion of the aristocratic Palaiologou-Benizelou family, the oldest in Athens, was once home to the city's patron saint. Agia (Saint) Filothei (1522–1589), whose actual name was Revoula, or Rygoula, was a force to be reckoned with who valiantly dedicated herself to those in need during the Ottoman Occupation.

The home (the original parts of which date back to the 16th–17th centuries with additions made in the late 1700s plus recent renovations) is today a museum, where visitors can admire the two-storey building, with its elegant marble-arched courtyard, the remains of a Roman wall, a wine press and olive press at the back and a fountain at the front.

Visitors can also watch a short documentary about Agia Filothei, although her story was a lot more dramatic and eventful than the film reveals. Married off to a much older man at the age of 14, the young Revoula suffered years of abuse from her husband before he dropped dead while smoking a hookah at a men's coffeeshop. In 1551, she chose God over her prestigious suitors and received the name Filothei (Friend of God). She made it her mission – despite the many life-threatening risks involved – to turn her home into what she described as a 'Parthenon' for the needy; a shelter for both Christian and Muslim women, destined for the harem, whom she rescued and educated in crafts. She also set up secret religious schools and hospices for the elderly, orphaned and poor. Near her home in Plaka she created a monastery (today the Archdiocese of Athens) that catered to the sick and destitute.

Inevitably her actions made her a top target for the Turks. They arrested and tortured her in October 1588 at the church of Agios Andreas, strapping her to a column and leaving her for dead. Her sister nuns found her and took her home, where she died from her wounds four months later.

Address Adrianou 96, Plaka, Athens 10556, +30 210 3248861 | Getting there Metro to Monastiraki (M1 & M3) | Hours Tue–Thu 10am–1pm, Sun 11am–4pm | Tip Next door to the mansion you'll find The Loom, a store stacked full of magnificently hand-woven rugs, materials, cushion covers and bed linen in traditional and artful styles.

# 18 Bios Rooftop Bar
*More than drinks with a stunning Acropolis view*

Pioneering in both its style and concept since it opened in 2003, Bios is a multimedia-obsessed multi-cultural space that collaborates with artists and trailblazers from Greece and around the world, hosting everything from experimental electronica gigs and DJ sets to theatre workshops, digital installations and children's plays. Its characteristic interior soaks up the vibes from the area it's situated in, on the border between Gazi and Kerameikos – one of mixed cultures, new art, a palpitant urbanity and dingy industrial architecture that's slowly but surely undergoing gentrification. Its downstairs bar with mismatched furniture and a giant lit-up vintage Aeroflot sign over the bar suggests the artsy, intellectual and playful character of its organisers and clientele – who range from the loyal to the curious.

The rooftop's ambience is modish and cool but also easy-going and unpretentious – striped sun loungers, metallic beer-barrel seats, a wooden stage-bench and large light cubes blend the digital age and gritty urbanity with an upbeat beach mood. The latter is further emphasised also by their refreshing famous Papoto ice lollies, based on cocktails such as the margarita, piña colada and daiquiri, and served in a glass of crushed ice.

Although there are several lovely rooftop bars to choose from to soak up heartening views of the illuminated Parthenon and Lycabettus Hill, if you're looking for a more local hangout and want to combine your vista-flavoured drink with more than a sit-down chat experience, Bios always has a multimedia-inspired card up its sleeve: from film screenings that you can follow wearing wireless headphones loaned from the bar, to live installations, an eclectic programme of opera and theatre of many kinds, music gigs and audio 'journeys' by top DJs (themed on the sunset or full moon), this scenic rooftop certainly offers more than one view.

Address Pireos 84, Gazi, Athens 10435, +30 210 3425335, www.bios.gr | Getting there Metro to Kerameikos (M 3) or Thissio (M 1) | Hours Daily 11 – 4am | Tip Stop off at Technopolis, the city's old gasworks centre (you'll spot it from its characteristic red tower and barrel-like buildings) turned cultural space, café and municipal radio station. In daytime hours, you can also visit its museum. In May it hosts the month-long, open-air European Jazz Festival.

# 19 Black Duck Garden

*Taking tea at the (former) palace*

The wrought-iron gates behind the formal entrance to the Black Duck Garden aren't quite what you imagined as a time machine's portal, yet they usher you from the city-centre bustle of 21st-century Athens to the stillness of a 19th-century parlour – and a royal one at that. There's also a more romantic entry through a short arcade that opens straight into the delightful garden for taking refreshments on balmy days.

Completed in 1833, this graceful neoclassical mansion was one of the first mansions built in Athens after it was named capital of modern Greece. The Chian banker Stamatis Vouros made it available to newly installed King Otto and Queen Amalia as their temporary palace during the six years it took to build their permanent residence. Amalia loved gardens and set to work creating one here, too – albeit a smaller version of the National Gardens that are her legacy to the city. The original garden extended across the entire square but was scaled back through the years by urban development. All that remains today is the interior courtyard where Amalia and Otto probably took their tea, as well as some of the original fixtures, including plants and a small tiered fountain.

Indoors, the ambience – if not all of the original antique furniture – has also been preserved in this bistro-style café. You can almost picture Amalia reaching for a hard-bound volume of poetry from the alcove library as tea is served. The setting's authenticity is easily verified by popping into the adjacent Museum of the City of Athens that occupies a second mansion Vouros built for his brother.

Occasional poetry or literary readings add to the salon atmosphere. The décor wonderfully blends ornate antiques with modern minimalism like velvet upholstery and chrome fixtures. It's the perfect place to take time out from the city's contemporary tensions and ponder life in slower times.

Address Ioannou Paparrigopoulou 5–7, Plateia Klafthmonos, Athens 10561, +30 210 3252396 | Getting there Metro to Panepistimio (M2); bus 1, 2, 4, 11, 12, 15 or 227 | Hours Daily 10–2am | Tip *The Poets*, a painting by Giorgio de Chirico's mentor Georgios Roilos, adorns the foyer of the Parnassus Literary Society on Plateia Karytsi behind the café.

# 20__ The Blue Condo
*The fading flagship building of a new Athens*

The Blue Condo framing the upper end of Exarchia Square is an urban landmark. Built in the early 1930s, this 40-apartment complex was a symbol of the new, modern city emerging in the interwar period. It wasn't just its colour – sky blue – or architectural lines that caused even the famed architect Le Corbusier to exclaim '*c'est très beau*', but the concept of urban living that it embodied. This modern vibe was reflected in its residents, a mix of artists, intellectuals and actors, including Oscar winner Katina Paxinou.

The building's mission was to present city dwelling as similarly communal to village life, with shared living spaces like a rooftop garden and swimming pool, laundry room, dryers powered by the steam from the central heating, and lounges. Apartments also featured amenities such as built-in cupboards and kitchen appliances imported from Switzerland; few apartments today come equipped with a refrigerator, much less in 1934. Art deco flourishes survive, from the iconic black-and-white tiled floors to the porthole windows in the flat double-wood doors.

By virtue of its location in the city centre, especially the views from its terrace, the Blue Condo could not escape the impending war or civil war that followed. As several of its eminent residents were involved in the Nazi resistance, the building was reportedly used as a contact point for underground groups, most notably Midas 614, which maintained links with the Allies. In the civil war, it was a base for the Left forces, which briefly installed a machine gun on the roof. Bullet holes from the December 1944 battles are still visible in the marble steps leading from the lobby.

Like the neighbourhood it dominates, the Blue Condo has taken a real battering in recent years, the vivid blue colour fading to a murky grey as it teeters on the edge between gentrification and decay, a symbol of the stubborn defiance that characterises the neighborhood.

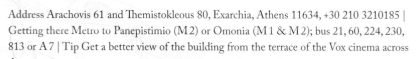

Address Arachovis 61 and Themistokleous 80, Exarchia, Athens 11634, +30 210 3210185 | Getting there Metro to Panepistimio (M 2) or Omonia (M 1 & M 2); bus 21, 60, 224, 230, 813 or A 7 | Tip Get a better view of the building from the terrace of the Vox cinema across the street.

# 21 The Chess Café

*Neither lies nor fancy coffee at the Panellinion*

For a *kafeneion*, it is uncharacteristically quiet. But patrons don't come to Panellinion to argue over politics or football (or both simultaneously as in many cases the two are inextricable). Nor do they come to indulge in the counter-culture ambience of other area cafés. They come to play chess. And every single table in the café is set up with a chess set, ready for the contest.

Panellinion isn't the sort of place that attracts passersby. Scuffed tables, a marble mosaic floor typical of 1950s and 1960s kitchens, stiff wooden chairs with flaking paint, and, at first glance, a clientele of mostly pensioners. The coffee is almost exclusively *Ellinikos*, individually brewed over a gas flame. The décor is mostly framed photos, including one of the original, far grander premises at the corner of Benaki Street that it occupied for the first eight decades after its founding in 1885. Pride of place among these souvenirs of its history is a magazine spread from 24 August, 1992, featuring Gary Kasparov, the Russian former world chess champion, who not only stopped by Panellinion but simultaneously played – and won – 30 games against the café's regulars.

Chess isn't just a game, but a philosophy. Or, as the Emanuel Lasker quote tacked to the service counter notes, 'On the chessboard lies and hypocrisy do not survive long.' As a game, it enjoys enduring popularity in Greece, with active clubs throughout the country. Panellinion is more of a haven, a place where players go to share their love of the game, rather than compete for a title. Like the décor, this love for chess has remained steady over time. Perhaps the one thing that has changed is that the coffee house no longer charges customers by the hour so they can continue to contemplate the board without anxiety about running up a bill. And there's no rush to leave: Panellinion will stay open until the final checkmate. checkmate, even if it takes hours. Unlike our fast-paced lives, chess requires strategy and patience.

Address Mavromichali 16, Athens 10680, +30 210 3634492 | Getting there Metro to Panepistimio (M 2); bus 21, 22, 54, 60, 100, 224, 608, 622 or 732 | Hours Daily 8am–9pm (or later) | Tip The old antenna atop the Law School Library on the corner of Solonos was used for Morse code transmissions to the government-in-exile in Cairo in World War II.

# 22 Cine Thision

*Silver screen under a golden Parthenon*

Cine Thision, the capital's first open-air cinema, has resolutely retained its original local, traditional, old-fashioned charm. Opened in 1935 for summer screenings, it offers a heartening view of the Parthenon, that you can watch slowly light up in golden light shortly after sundown, and remains off the mainstream radar.

Unlike the Greek psyche, during World War II, the cinema survived unscathed as occupying German forces put it to good use for screening propaganda films. Since then it has undergone several small renovations, such as screening digitally and adding surround sound, but essentially it would still be recognisable to a time traveller from the '30s.

Showing two films every night, sometimes beloved old classics from a bygone era of the silver screen (always subtitled in Greek) that enhance through their nostalgic glamour the ambience of Athens' dying summer cinema tradition, it is open from May to October. Surrounded by greenery and caressed by a gentle breeze carrying the delightful summer aromas of basil and jasmine, viewers seat themselves on red chairs under the stars, laying snacks on little round tables. During the cooler months, blankets are available to keep you feeling comfortable. Unlike any other cinema in Athens, the old-style canteen, decorated with old projectors and film star posters, serves *tsipouro* (Greek firewater made from distilled grapes) or organic local wine, *bottarga* from Mesolonghi where the owners are from, freshly baked cheese pie, and several products made from sour cherries – liqueur, spoon sweet (syrupy stewed fruit eaten with a spoon) and *vyssinada* (fruit syrup stirred into cold water). Local cats will helpfully clean up any food that might get dropped on the ground.

The romance of the cinema has even inspired couples to propose marriage there, and the cinema has hosted a couple of wedding parties.

Address Apostolou Pavlou 7, Thissio, Athens 11851, +30 210 3420864, www.cinethisio.gr |
Getting there Metro to Thissio (M1) | Hours Depends on sunset – films usually start at
9pm | Tip Just five minutes' walk away is the National Observatory of Athens on the Hill
of the Nymphs where you can pre-book a night tour or simply walk up to and enjoy
glittering views of the city.

# 23 Cinque Wine Bar

*Five could be your lucky number tonight*

'Wine is constant proof that God loves us and loves to see us happy.' These words hang framed next to the entrance to this tiny bar. With room for only 16 people inside and 15 outside, chances are you're going to be happy not just sipping but making friends with your neighbours as well as the staff. What sets Cinque apart is the cosy personal touch and genuine hospitality.

As owner Evangelia Prassou says, 'We are wine lovers and so we know how to approach other wine lovers. We take them on a tour of Greek wine regions, and by talking to them, we help them choose which of our 45 labels they'd like to taste. We offer 19 tasting combinations but we can also make them up to suit the customer. We only deal with small Greek producers and we serve mostly Greek varieties. Did you know there are 300 native grapes, and more than 3,200 labels!'

Most of these have appeared in the last 20 years, and faced with names like Romeo and Juliet, Two Rivers, Partridge in the Vines and Mega Spileo, one really needs a guide. The wine list makes good reading while you wait, yielding such nuggets as 'xinomavro is a tricky devil in the vineyard … and can result in acidic plonk'.

With Evangelia and her husband Grigoris, a sommelier, advising you, there's no such danger. They opened their first wine bar in Lamia, but moved to Athens in 2015 when their son, Nikitas, enrolled in university here to study oenology. The place was an instant success and will help fund his further studies abroad, the main object of their venture.

The three pay the same attention to the food served to complement the wines, sourcing the cheeses, cold meats and other delicious snacks only from small producers. They've even come up with vegan cheese. But why cinque? 'Because we first fell in love with wines in Italy, cinque represents the five taste sensations, and by spinning the number 5 we found our logo.'

Address 15 Agatharchou, Psyrri, Athens 10554, +30 215 5017853, www.cinque.gr | Getting there Metro to Thissio (M1) or Monastiraki (M1 & M3) and a 10-minute walk | Hours Mon–Sat 6pm–midnight | Tip If you need loud music, the joints next door supply plenty of it.

# 24 Daphni Monastery
*Rising like a phoenix for 2,000 years*

This World Heritage monument, whose church has some of the most stunning mosaics in Greece, has been under almost constant repair since its beginnings. The plot, once a laurel wood, first held a temple dedicated to Apollo Daphnephoros (the laurel bearer). That was destroyed in 395 A.D. by barbarians, all but a few Ionic columns, which were incorporated into the first monastery erected in its place in the 6th century. Only one is left; Lord Elgin made off with the rest, which have been replaced with obvious too-white marble copies.

Despite its prestige, it was later abandoned until the 11th century, when someone high up in the Byzantine imperial court restored it, building a new church and lining it with ravishing mosaics. But with the nefarious Fourth Crusade in 1204, Crusaders took over the Byzantine empire and the monastery became part of the Duchy of Athens, run by Cistercians. The sarcophagi near the entrance belong to two Catholic dukes.

Semi-abandoned once more under the Ottomans, it was variously used as a garrison, a base for Greek revolutionaries, a Bavarian barracks, and a lunatic asylum as well as a monastery. In our day, though, owing to earthquake damage, it has been closed for repairs for decades and has only recently become visitable again.

Worth seeing are the crenellated battlements of its outer walls, the cloisters on either side and the superb mosaics – of the Life of Christ and the Virgin, the saints and prophets – dominated by the piercing eyes and stern face of the Pantocrator (Ruler of All) in the golden dome. There's no doubt he knows your secrets. But take your binoculars because, except for the flowers above the north door, most of the mosaics are too high to examine properly. Many gaps reflect the church's chequered history, but it's a miracle any survived. There was even an attempt to melt down the tesserae for their gold.

**Address** Athinon, Haidari 12400, +30 210 5811558 | **Getting there** Metro to Agia Marina (M 3) and then bus 811; buses from Athens A 16, C 16 or 836, or from Piraeus 801 or 845 | **Hours** Tue & Fri 8am – 3pm | **Tip** At the Haidari 'death' camp just beyond the monastery, hundreds were executed by the Nazis in 1944 in reprisals for partisan attacks against them. It was the most notorious prison in Greece.

# 25 The Digital Museum
*A high-tech introduction to an ancient philosopher*

Much disappointment has been expressed (especially by Greeks) about how undermined the area of Plato's Academy is. After all, the argument goes, what looks today like a park with a few measly ruins scattered around, was among the world's first and most influential schools of philosophy on which modern civilisation is founded, and should be presented in a more meritorious manner. Founded in 387 B.C. by Plato, the Academy was an entire district located 1.5 km northwest of the city centre, beside an olive grove dedicated to the goddess Athena, itself a sacred site. It was organised into several schools, mainly centred on dialectic exchange, mathematics and philosophy.

Today, the expanses of parkland areas are chiefly visited by local dog walkers, although a few tourists make the extra effort to leave the city centre to traipse in awe where Plato once taught. Many visitors are unaware, however, that there is a fascinating Digital Museum (since 2015) on the site, created by the Foundation of the Hellenic World (which offers interactive, virtual time travel in their Tholos). The space, which looks like a shipping container, offers a highly informative tour via hi-tech, interactive media including digital screens, texts, maps and digital applications such as a computer game and video projections.

Plato said: 'You can discover more about a person in an hour of play than in a year of conversation,' and the museum embodies that very concept. It is separated into three rooms: the first introduces the critical role of Plato and the Academy he created, also depicting how the area once physically appeared; the second introduces his intellectual methodologies and invites you to explore your own thought processes; and the third showcases how Plato's imperative teachings were spread by his followers through time, and how they continue to impact the world today.

Address Corner of Monastiriou & Kreontos, Akadimia Platonos, Athens 10442, +30 210 5142138, www.plato-academy.gr | Getting there Bus 051 to Kratilou or Kete from Omonia Square – both stops are in the central part of the Plato Academy sites | Hours Tue–Sun 9am–4pm | Tip Have coffee with members of The European Village non-profit community (Monastiriou 140), who actively organise everything from yoga and theatre workshops to a non-GMO seed exchange.

# 26 — Diomedes Botanical Garden

*The biggest in the eastern Med yet known to so few*

It covers 186 hectares but only 20 of them are landscaped and planted. The oldest pine forest in Attica accounts for the rest, along with 500 spontaneous plants, what gardeners call 'volunteers'. There are 15 large flower beds, 25 pools with aquatic plants (and frogs and turtles), an arboretum with trees from all six continents including Oceania, a nursery, greenhouse and herbarium with 12,000 dried species and a seedbank containing 800 varieties. But Athenians on the other side of town will not have heard of it, much less visited.

Athens has so few green spaces and most of them exist because they are either too steep to build on or surround some ancient monument or relic. In the Diomedes garden, the only antiquities are alive. Here, in the historic plants section, you can see species mentioned by Theophrastus, who created the world's first botanical garden in the 4th century B.C., Dioscorides, the Bible and mythology, such as the hemlock (*Conium maculatum*) which Socrates drank to end his life or the giant fennel (*Ferula communis*) in which Prometheus concealed the fire he stole from Mount Olympus to bestow on humanity.

The garden itself was a gift to the University of Athens by Alexander N. Diomedes and his wife Julia upon his death in 1950. He was a polymath educated abroad, a close associate of Venizelos, politician and president of the National Bank. His longest job was President of the Bank of Greece, founded in the 1930s to keep the country's finances separate from its politics at a time when Greece was both bankrupt and destabilised by refugees as it is today. He and Julia, from a wealthy Alexandrian family, married too late to have children. She was a passionate gardener, known to fly in new varieties of roses from abroad.

They decided to leave part of their fortune to create this garden and, in her memory, it includes at least 100 types of rose.

Address Iera Odos 401, Haidari 12461, +30 210 5811557, +30 210 5812582, +30 210 5813049, www.diomedes-bg.uoa.gr | Getting there Metro to Agia Marina (M 3) and bus 811, buses from Athens A16, G16, 836 or from Piraeus 801, 845 | Hours Mon–Fri 8am–sunset, Sat, Sun & most holidays 10am–sunset, closed 15 July–31 Aug | Tip The Iera Odos follows the route of the ancient Sacred Way that led from the centre of Athens near the Kerameikos cemetery to the Eleusis, the shrine of Demeter, where the 'mysteries' took place, the world's best-kept secret.

# 27 Diporto
*Two doors into the underworld*

Graffiti and grime mark the entrance to this taverna, and two gaping doors in the pavement. Peer down either door and all you'll see are a couple of steep flights of steps leading to a dark basement. On one side a marble sink, on the other a table or two, and if you cock your head, a wall lined with aged oaken wine barrels will greet your vision. You might also get a whiff of frying fish or simmering beans. The pong of salt cod, which can be as off-putting as a teenager's sneakers, may make you withdraw and head for a safe bakery or falafel joint to sate your hunger pangs.

But if you dare descend to this underground eatery, you'll find yourself in one of Athens' oldest tavernas. Although it's known as Diporto and has been in existence since 1887, there is no sign bearing the name, while the listed building above it dates from 1875. This is one of the few places left where you can drink real retsina, and where the barrels are not simply an empty echo of the past.

And if you should choose to eat here, you may have to share a table – there are only eight – and break (real peasant) bread with the Mayor of Athens, foreign celebrities or local men and women who work in the Central Market a block away. Barba Mitsos, the owner, started as a waiter when he was 12, and still serves the most delectable chickpeas, anchovies gently stewed with tomatoes, beans, fried cod with garlic sauce and other simple Greek classics. Clad in a spotless white jacket, with his white hair and white beard, he may also produce a photo of Francis Ford Coppola or tell you about the Communist poet Kostas Varnalis, a Lenin-prize winner, whose photo hangs on the wall.

If you're up to it (or perhaps down to it), Diporto will give you a glimpse of Athens 50 years ago. But don't expect a menu. Get up and choose from the pots in the kitchen in the same room or point to what others are savouring.

Address Sokratous 9 and Theatrou (in the city centre), +30 210 3211463 | Getting there Metro to Omonia (M1 & M2) or Monastiraki (M1 & M3) | Hours Mon–Sat 8am–7pm | Tip An itinerant vendor has his wares spread out on the pavement outside Diporto, but some are hung on the wall: a bugle, a French horn and a trumpet.

# 28 Dirty Cherubs
*The city's most vandalised outdoor sculpture*

There's a Greek proverb that says it's better to lose an eye than get a bad name. And this certainly fits the fate of a somewhat baroque sculpted fountain dubbed the most vandalised outdoor sculpture in the city.

The fountain, perennially dry, sits in the middle of a small tree-shaded square almost opposite the sprawling Pedion Areos, or Field of Mars. City cleaning crews are routinely tasked with cleaning the spray-painted scribbles and swirls of political and football graffiti that have turned the three-tiered marble sculpture into a bulletin board for discontent. The dolphin-shaped spouts at the base seem to draw football vandals, while politics literally covers the upper tiers. Even the three trumpet-blowing cherubs grouped atop the third tier are often covered in angry scrawls. As a result, much of the surface marble has been eroded and some of the ornamentation has been chipped or broken off.

The fountain sculptor is as unknown as the park it occupies, whose sole claim to fame as the backdrop for a scene from the 1969 comedy *Poios Thanassis* (*Who is Thanassis*) starring Thanassis Vengos was lost when the square, Thymarakia, was renamed in honour of 'Argentinian Democracy'. The fountain was installed here in 1962 by the City of Athens, which had salvaged it, among other pieces, from the 'Little Palace' or Palataki, that used to serve as a country retreat for King George I. The estate, which included stables and an olive press, featured a two-storey towered mansion and is decorated with murals by Nikiforos Lytras and Nikolaos Gyzis, two of Greece's most celebrated 19th-century painters. It's assumed that the fountain's sculptor was one of the numerous guests invited to the estate by its original owner, who had a penchant for the arts. Today, the building houses the public library of Haidari, an outer district of metropolitan Athens.

Address Plateia Argentinis Dimokratias, Leoforos Alexandras, Athens 11472 | Getting there Bus 14, 18, 19, 21, 230 or 813 | Tip The Fournos Art Theatre on nearby Mavromichali is the city's leading venue for experimental children's theatre, with an emphasis on digital arts.

# 29 Doorway to Mystical Urban Legend

*And Athens' esoteric past*

Even when it was first built in 1870, the house on Akadimias 58A stood out among Athens' other prestigious residences for the metal dragon that roared at passers-by from its first-floor balcony. The legendary creature, an unorthodox symbol in Greece, has now fled, but the house, built as the home of Saxon architect Ernst Ziller, who was commissioned to design some of Greece's most impressive neoclassical buildings, continues to draw curious observers. It's not just the building's narrow façade and the Gothic-medieval black metal door leading into the house's side entrance that have generated curiosity, but all the stories that have been spun over the last century regarding what really went on in the three-storey building.

In 1923, the home came under the ownership of Greek banker Dionysios P. Loverdos, who filled its rooms with his extensive and expensive collection of rare Byzantine art. Religiously themed furnishings, icons, wall mosaics, frescoes and even an ornate temple-room made up the banker's personal museum-home, which was donated to the country's Byzantine and Christian Museum in 1979.

Briefly opening to the public as a museum and gallery space, the home's contents were soon after removed and the unique building was abandoned, as it still remains to this day, (illegally) becoming the stomping ground for investigators, photographers, ghost hunters and occultists who insist that it was once the key meeting place for Athens' Teutonic Order, headed by Loverdos, with the temple room used as a ceremonial space for the cult's oath-taking. Another completely unproven but much-repeated theory is that there are underground chambers leading to the city's subterranean passageways, as well as odd characteristics such as missing tiles in the centre of many floors, making it one of Athens' greatest enigmas.

**Address** Akadimias 58A, Athens 10679 | **Getting there** Metro to Syntagma (M 2 & M 3); bus A 4, 026, B 2 or 230 | **Tip** Parallel to Akadimias, one street up is Merlin Street, where at number 1 (corner with 9 Vas. Sofias Avenue) you'll find the Theocharakis Foundation in a large neoclassical building. With themed cultural exhibitions, concerts and a cosy first-floor café, this makes for a great place to stop after you've pondered the mysterious doorway.

# 30_Eleni Marneri Galerie

*Modern Greek jewellery in an ethereal ambience*

Greeks have always loved their jewellery, worn throughout the millennia to embellish beauty, reflect social status and guard against evil. At several museums across the capital one can admire a multitude of examples from the Bronze, Mycenaean, Gold, Hellenistic and Byzantine Ages, but most visitors are unaware that they can also see a collection of the most contemporary jewellery made by Greek designers.

Located around the corner from the New Acropolis Museum in a tiny street you'd only find if you were lost, Eleni Marneri Galerie, named after its visionary owner, has for 30 years showcased modern Greek jewellery. Before even stepping into the urban, airy and elegant gallery your entry into a world of playful contrasts between past, present and future begins by looking through a glass floor under the shop's façade, where you'll see an ancient mosaic. The current building in fact stands on the foundations of a 'villa urbana' dated from the Late Geometric Period to Late Antiquity, parts of which can also be observed through the floor of the gallery.

There is an ethereal aura inside, created by a mix of the astounding yet harmoniously presented diversity of creative jewellery and other art pieces on show together with dreamy wafts of pure aromas like orange blossom and rose coming from a shelf of Florentine Santa Maria Novella fragrances. Intricate and modernist exhibits of all materials, some with sparkling stones like ruby, aquamarine or diamonds, all invite a closer look. Colourful aluminium sardines swim across a wall; everywhere you turn you'll be drawn in by pieces that express the contemporary vision and personal story of the artist who created it. All pieces, from space-age metals to elaborate paper feathers and from digital flowers to tribal wood are an *objet d'art* with a singular identity; many are also for sale. Free tours are provided.

Address Lebessi 5, Makriyanni, Athens 11742, +30 210 8619488, www.elenimarneri.com | Getting there Metro to Acropolis (M2) | Hours Tue, Thu & Fri 11am–8pm, Wed & Sat 11am–4pm | Tip Just a few doors down is Solebike, which takes you on educational, friendly audio (through headphones) tours on an electric bicycle for exploration of ancient and modern Athens.

# 31 Eridanos River

*An archaeological site inside a metro station*

For a unique but mesmerising experience step away from the drone, artificial lighting and rush of crowds in a metro station onto a glass bridge just seconds from the tracks where you can be still and immerse yourself in a tranquil ancient environment.

In a 300-square-metre expanse of archaeological excavations you'll find and hear the Eridanos river, flowing since the Mycenaean Era. Natural light fills the area, and birds flutter in to rest on ruins. One's imagination travels back to a time when Athens was covered in lush greenery, with rivers and streams, well laid-out buildings and shops.

A great variety of impressive artefacts, all presented in photographs and text at the site, were also unearthed here, along with the remains of residential buildings (dating from the 8th century B.C. to the 19th century). Unveiled to the public in 2008, this still unacknowledged section was the most impressive discovery made by the Attiko Metro company when building the underground system, although magnificent archaeological finds can also be admired at Acropolis, Syntagma and Kerameikos stations.

Flowing from the springs beneath Lycabettus Hill, north of the Acropolis, and through the Agora of Athens, the Eridanos reached Kerameikos cemetery (a tiny stream remains there today). The Ilissos, the other major river of ancient Athens (which flowed from Mount Hymettus) joined the Eridanos west of the Acropolis, pouring into the Kifissos river. Both the Eridanos and Ilissos, honoured by sculptures of river gods and water nymphs at the sides of the western pediment on the Parthenon, served as resources for many areas of Athenian life. The Eridanos provided fresh water for drinking, religious ceremonies and utilitarian functions, to being the refreshing backdrop for exercise and relaxing social gatherings, just as it continues to offer a magical moment of calm today.

Address Monastiraki Metro Station, Monastiraki Square, Athens 10563 | Getting there Any blue line metro or the HSAP green line | Hours Daily 6.30am – 11.30pm | Tip Head to Agias Eirinis Square five minutes away for the Loukoumades store, and tuck into Greece's answer to doughnuts, served with hot chocolate sauce and more.

# 32 Ermou's Milonga Mondays

*A weekly tango party under the stars*

One Monday night in 2009, Tango-lover Vassilis and his dance partner placed a small CD player on a ledge on a pedestrianised street and enjoyed an hour of alfresco Argentinian tango dancing. A week later they returned with friends to dance at the same spot, across from the ancient Kerameikos cemetery with a view of twinkling Lycabettus Hill above. Through word of mouth the weekly gathering began to attract tens and soon hundreds of tango dancers who flocked to the scene. Tango *aficionado* Giorgos Minadakis soon hopped on board, taking on the music organisation and buying a generator, sound system, giant speakers and a console.

It's quite spellbinding to arrive at the scene on the lower part of cobblestone-paved, greenery-ensconced Ermou, following the music that leads you away from the urban buzz of Thissio to discover a huge crowd of dancers from 18 to 80 years twirling, trotting and swaying with gusto. Whether you're an absolute beginner or an expert dancer, you're guaranteed to find a partner, especially if you are a woman, as men need expertise to lead. As an event that is welcomed by the neighbourhood (there are no shops or homes nearby), it has been taking place every Monday, rain or shine, with numbers surpassing 400 during the hottest months, for nine years.

In an ebullient and friendly ambience that welcomes all kinds of people, the party offers crisis-hit Greeks a welcome sense of community and expressive relief. Apart from an inherent love of drama that makes up the fibre of their being, the relatively novel infatuation with tango offers locals a healthy distraction from daily troubles. The appeal is obvious: there's no entry fee, and attendees are free to bring their own drinks to spend the first day of the working week dancing under the stars.

**Address** The bottom part of pedestrianised Ermou, across the bus depot and Kerameikos cemetery. Info: Giorgos Minadakis +30 693 6754351. | Getting there Metro to Thissio (M1) | Hours Daily 10.30pm – 3.30am | Tip Keep the party going by crossing over Pireos Street at the end of Ermou and exploring the vibrant nightlife of Gazi.

# 33 Exarchia Square

*A long tradition of antiestablishmentarianism*

Exarchia's reputation as a hotbed of anarchists, vandals and druggies has exploded beyond the nation's borders recently with increased protests, sometimes violent, against austerity measures and perceived injustices. But, in fact, the first protest took place in 1859 against King Otto and the district was a countercultural bastion from its infancy. This was a logical consequence of the presence, first of the city's University in 1841, followed by the schools of Philosophy, Law and Chemistry, and in 1873 the National Technical University, aka Athens Polytechnic (famous for the uprising 100 years later that precipitated the junta's unravelling).

Students are usually more liberal than the authorities, and universities tend to attract intellectuals, artists and other 'free spirits' who don't want to be bound by social conventions. You could compare Exarchia to Greenwich Village or the Latin Quarter of yore, with their cafés, bookshops, impromptu theatres, left-wing and 'long-hair' attitudes.

Athenians of a certain age who never go there think of it as lawless and dangerous. But young people and residents like the buzz and they also try to clean it up their way and squeeze out the junkies – creating a playground out of a vacant lot, opening a hangout where migrants can mingle with locals, erecting a basketball hoop on the square – and during 'troubles' neighbourhood tavernas and shops have nothing to fear though the police don't enter. The hoodies don't foul their own nest.

In the square at night you might find an Iranian grilling kebabs, a bonfire surrounded by dancers, people of all ages sipping beer on the ledges. And after a good protest, the statue in the centre of three cupids around a five-globe lamppost may be festooned with trophies, like riot police helmets and shields. 'It's like being in the eye of the storm,' says one habitué.

Address Exarchia Square, intersection of Themistokleous & Stournari, Athens 10681 |
Getting there Metro to Omonia (M 1 & M 2) and 10 minutes' walk; bus 035, 046, 060,
200, A 7 or B 7 | Tip Stournari is the cyber souk, while there are dozens of great eateries,
bars and music spots in the vicinity of the square.

# 34 The Exile Museum
*Personal artefacts and the 'art' of survival*

It looks like an ordinary note, scrawled on an odd scrap of paper until you realise it's a piece of fabric torn by a prisoner from his shirt to write a farewell note to his family while being ferried by his German captors to his execution. At first it seems out of place in a museum dedicated to internal exiles, the odious practice of rounding up and banishing dissenters to islands like Ai Stratis. But surrounded by other such pieces of people's lives and pain, it fits the story these artefacts tell – of a people united against a common foe, then divided against each other.

If you've visited Ai Stratis, it's hard to imagine that this beautiful Aegean island between Limnos and Lesvos was used to incarcerate political prisoners, first during the Metaxas dictatorship in the 1930s, at the end of the civil war, and even as late as the 1967–1974 years of the junta's rule. It wasn't only place of exile, but like Makronissos, the prison island where Leftists were sent for 'rehabilitation', it looms darkest in the Greek psyche.

Housed in a charming neoclassical building that was donated by the government in 2003, the Exile Museum is known mainly to history students as a research centre. But as more of the personal items donated by former exiles and their families are put on display, it is shaping into a unique museum, one tasked with the uncomfortable mission of exhibiting a history that many people would much rather forget. There's the wedding dress of a bride who was executed before she wore it, a chess set made from bread, a shirt ripped and bloodied during torture. But mostly there's the art – sketches, paintings, small ornaments and scraps of poetry that detainees created to reclaim and retain their humanity. These works, many by now-noted artists, provide a visual description of life in exile – perhaps the most important documentation in the Ai Stratis archive. And of course these experiences inform the works of artists like Tassos, widely exhibited in Greece and abroad.

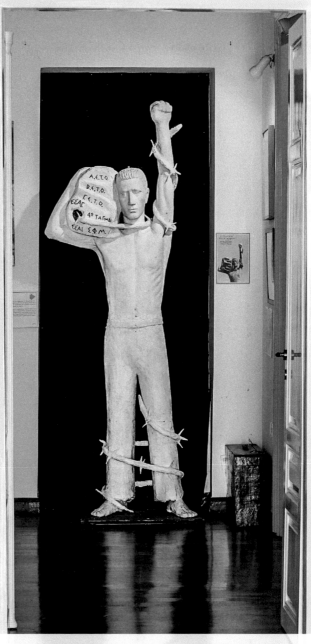

Address Agion Asomaton 31, Thissio, Athens 10553, +30 210 3213488 | Getting there Metro to Thissio (M1); bus 25, 26, 54, 227, 813 or 815 | Hours Tue–Fri 10am–1pm, Sat & Sun 11am–2pm | Tip If you stroll between the Thissio metro station and Monastiraki, you'll want to check out the vendors with their off-beat arts and crafts along the way.

# 35__Fatsio

*A taste of the 1970s' urban middle class*

The Italian-sounding name in red neon and embroidered half-window curtains deceptively conjure up a *trattoria* because Fatsio is pure 'old' Athens, distilling the flavour of the Greek capital's post-war bourgeois class in a menu as untouched by time as the décor.

Fatsio has occupied the same Pangrati premises since 1969, bucking the trend for establishments to change style or name or both. Arriving in Greece in the mid-1960s, Georgios Fatsios brought with him the reputation of his popular Istanbul eatery, funnelling his experiences into creating one of the fashionable 'continental-style' restaurants. The atmosphere has been preserved virtually intact by his son; blink fast and you might think you're back in the early 1970s.

Don't expect fancy or fashionable dishes. The menu is part of the ambience. Fatsio is like a time capsule and if the red tablecloths, high-backed chairs and art deco murals aren't hint enough, perusing the heated glass-cased buffet makes the point. Standards from the *polítiki* (Greek Istanbul) cuisine like artichokes in a thick lemon sauce, *soutzoukakia* (oval meatballs simmered in piquant tomato sauce) and stewed beef wrapped in aubergine are complemented by Wiener schnitzel or *noua* (beef silverside) in gravy – dishes popular among the old Athenian middle class – and pans of *tyropita* made with a béchamel base and thin phyllo, then cut into squares. And there's always fish: fresh, usually pan-stewed, and served, as manners dictate, with home-made mayonnaise. The flavours are as subdued as the setting, a quiet dining hall where voices do not rise above the volume needed to carry them across the table.

Fatsio may seem dated but its charm hasn't faded – nor have its patrons. Regulars are a mix of retired diplomats or professors and politicians, writers, and locals – many of whom trace the tradition of Sunday lunch at Fatsio to their childhood.

Address Efroniou 5, Athens 11634, +30 210 7217421 | Getting there Metro to Evangelismos (M 3); bus 54, 203, 204, 250 or 732 | Hours Daily 11am – 6pm | Tip The Greek poet Kostas Varnalis, a regular, lived around the corner at Sp. Mercouri 27 for the last 17 years of his life.

# 36 Fokianos Sports Park

*Where athletes trained for the 1896 Olympics*

Even the less athletically inclined may harbour an Olympic fantasy or two – and Fokianos Sports Park is definitely the place to indulge it. Located across from the Panathenaic Stadium that hosted the revival of the ancient Games in 1896, this public sports facility is named after the man who trained Greece's first modern Olympians: Ioannis Fokianos. You don't even need to change into shorts to power-walk around the track and imagine entering the stadium to the sound of cheers.

A central location is part of the park's appeal. The other is its casual, open atmosphere which is less rigorous (and less intimidating) than a gym. No doubt many of the philosophies outlined in the late 19th century by Fokianos in his seminal manual on physical education are at work in the indoor-outdoor gym bearing his name, with the oversized chess 'board' providing the mental exercise to complement the physical workouts offered by the climbing wall, 50 m and 200 m tracks, cycling piste and trampoline. There are also basketball courts that convert to volleyball courts or five-a-side football pitches, plus an indoor gym for yoga, Pilates, martial arts and fencing. A team of trainers is committed to lifelong involvement in sport so there's no age group that isn't welcome for ad hoc workouts or personalised programmes, but like many visitors you can just walk in off the street and jog around the track.

Fokianos isn't just about working up a sweat. It's also about fun (there's a sand pit and tree house) and education (an exhibition focused on the early modern Olympics is growing into a small sports history museum). The café has a surprisingly extensive menu and has become a popular venue for hosting birthday parties. Indeed, the Fokianos Sports Park is a great place to visit with children, who will enjoy a few hours of play while parents get in a workout or just bask in the Athenian sun.

**Address** Leoforos Vassilissis Olgas 1, Athens 10557, +30 210 3233973 | **Getting there** Tram (all lines); bus 2, 4, 10, 11 or 550 | **Hours** Daily 8am–10pm | **Tip** The city's first fountain, a massive belle-époque construction in Zappeion, was a gift in the 1930s from the New York City-based Ulen Water Co.

# 37 __ Folk Music Museum

*The sound of Greek culture through the ages*

Most visitors who see Fivos Anoyanakis' collection of 1,200 Greek folk music instruments enthusiastically describe the experience as a 'great surprise'. Located in a renovated 1842 mansion in Plaka, the small museum (with a garden where large tortoises are part of the museum's family) is neither touristy nor customary. Its three levels eloquently present an incredible variety of instruments categorised by the sound vibration they create (membranophones, idiophones, aerophones and chordophones).

There's plenty of written information as well as photo and video presentations from various eras and different parts of Greece that offer visitors a deeper understanding of the instruments, their use and history. But the most exciting aspect is that you can listen to the sound of each instrument being played through headphones placed by each of the exhibits. You therefore discover not only how the instruments sound but also the kind of music they create – transporting the listener to different regions and moods – from goat-stomach bagpipes typically played in an alpine village to the baglama guitar used in a smoky rebetiko basement performance. Essentially via the instruments, many of them beautifully hand-crafted from an assortment of materials and colours and some carved with beautiful designs, you are taken on a journey through Greece's cultural heritage through its music.

A dedicated music lover, Anoyanakis donated his vast collection to the Greek state after 50 passionate years of learning, researching and writing about music. Starting as a violin student, he later became a renowned music critic for the Greek press while continuously researching modern and traditional Greek music genres and traditional instruments. Anything but an armchair music *aficionado*, he conducted extensive field research nationwide, bringing home recordings of academic and scientific use.

Address Diogenous 1–3, Plaka, Athens 10556, +30 210 3250198, www.melt.gr |
Getting there Metro to Thissio (M3) or Monastiraki (M1 & M3) | Hours Tue–Sun
8am–3pm | Tip Recently reopened to the public after 200 years is the octagonal
marble Tower of the Winds, the world's first weather station from 2,000 years ago.
How it worked remains a mystery, as its mechanism was looted during the Roman era.

# 38 Ghika's Studio

*A room without a view but still a masterpiece*

Nikos Hadjikyriakos-Ghikas (1906–1994) may not be a household name to foreigners but he was one of Greece's finest 20th-century artists. In his paintings, you'll see shapes that remind you of Braque, Picasso and Matisse, friends from his Paris days, absorbed into a style that is uniquely his own. But despite having travelled the world, and having homes in London, Hydra and Corfu, as well as Athens, one of his favourite subjects was his own studio.

This was not a starving artist's garret and he lavished a perfectionist's attention on every detail of this top floor of his Athens flat. Surprisingly, it lacks a view. Its large window looks onto a fire escape, but to Ghika that was an advantage. 'My personality and my laziness seem to prefer closed spaces. Just by letting my eyes fall on one spot or another, I will discover something,' he wrote. 'Hence the numerous still lifes … studios and interiors in my work.'

But before he allowed himself to paint, he had the walls of the old family flat stripped and rebuilt using old perforated bricks and cement blocks, leaving structural elements unplastered, but softened by white or grey wash, additional holes and special surface treatment. As a backdrop for his vast library or paintings, they are both neutral yet with a life of their own.

Ghika could hardly be termed lazy. Once finished with the studio, he decorated the rest of the flat with exceptional taste, mixing local objects with Japanese snuffboxes, European antiques, images of Buddha, bright silk cushions and many of his own paintings and sculptures, including a series of eye-stopping exotic masks.

During his life, he had over 50 exhibitions. But when did he have time to be so prolific? The lower floors of the building are filled with memorabilia and art from his friends, virtually everyone of any repute in the golden age of post-war Greece, including an Oscar from *Zorba the Greek* and poet Odysseas Elytis' Nobel Prize.

Address Kriezotou 3, Athens 10671, +30 210 3615702, 210 3630818, www.benaki.gr |
Getting there Metro to Syntagma (M2 & M3) and a three-minute walk | Hours Fri &
Sat 10am–6pm | Tip The Mastiha Shop on the corner specialises in products, edible,
drinkable and cosmetic, made with the precious resin from a tree that grows only in
southern Chios in the northeast Aegean.

# 39___Govosti

*Historic publishers of modern Greek literature*

The storefront on the narrow, graffiti-pocked street cutting through Exarchia may be its window to readers, but the fact that Govosti is a book publisher rather than seller is indicated by the opening hours, which end at 3pm. In its 90-plus years, Govosti has made enough of a mark on Greek publishing to earn a little eccentricity, having not only introduced the Russian writers to it but also published Greece's most acclaimed authors. Indeed, the hand-drawn logo (clearly informed by the aesthetic of Soviet art) is more familiar to readers than many authors' names.

Kostas Govostis moonlighted his way into publishing, producing his first book – Fyodor Dostoyevsky's 1877 short story *The Dream of a Ridiculous Man* – in 1926, at age 22 in his home. By 1936, the fledgling publishing house had grown into a small enterprise that moved into basement premises on Kanningos Square and added a book-binding unit. Politics coloured the enterprise from the start and, in turn, shaped generations of Greek readers. The focus on Russian literature and Marxist writers drew Greek intellectuals, imbuing the publishing house with a literary aura as writers like Mimis Karagatsis, Napoleon Lapathiotis, Angelos Sikelianos, Kostas Varnalis, Nikos Engonopoulos and Yannis Ritsos regularly met there. But Govostis' politics landed him in trouble with the Metaxas dictatorship; he was jailed and the entire stock of books burned.

But that was not the end of Govostis and his business. In 1951, he was first to use the single-accent system – a move both politically progressive and controversial because of the class implications of the simpler system. Following his death in 1958, the business has remained in the family, with a new generation bringing in new ideas, like Saturday morning 'salons' with tsipouro instead of tea. But even today's sleek, modern look cannot shake off the dust of history.

Address Zoodohou Pigis 73, Athens 10681, +30 210 3822251 | Getting there Metro to Panepistimio (M 2); bus 11, 290, A 2 or A 3 | Hours Mon–Fri 9am–3pm | Tip Stop to view the unusual Renaissance-style icons at the mid-19th-century church of Zoodohos Pigi (Life-Giving Source) at the Akadimias end of the street.

# 40__ The Greek Film Archive

*Preserving golden memories from the silver screen*

What does a profiterole have to do with Greek politics? A clue can be found on the walls of the Greek Film Archive where a still of a broke professor miming the dessert to a waiter hangs among other iconic Greek movie images that fuel scores of memes commenting on the social and political issues of the day.

Greek identity is anchored to the past. Even pop culture is rooted in the films of the 1950s and 1960s, and in the Instagram-paced present, is as good as antiquity. It's not nostalgia that makes films like *Beating Hearts at School Desks* resonate with Greeks across generations, but rather that the protagonists and their problems in the black-and-white films of Greek cinema's so-called golden age continue to provide metaphors for today's experiences, even to younger generations of Greeks weaned on American TV. This is why the Greek Film Archive isn't just a repository for 4,000 Greek and foreign films, 2,000 movie stills, and 5,000 original posters, scripts, costumes and props; it's a mirror of Greek society that reflects both its recent past and its present, a pop culture that aspires to the cinema of auteurs like Nikos Koundouros and Theodoros Angelopoulos but delights in the sassiness and antics of comedians like Thanassis Vengos.

Founded in 1950 by the Union of Athens Film Critics, the Greek Film Archive is part repository and part film institute. Today it is housed in the Lais cinema.

The 600-seat theatre was akin to a multiplex when it was built in 1948, but fell into ruin as television's spread kept audiences home. Ironically, TV saved the movies, but doomed theatres like Lais, which thanks to the Archive has been renovated into a cultural centre that hosts regular festival screenings as well as researchers. The 2,000-square-metre premises occupy four levels, including a rooftop terrace used for open-air screenings in the summer.

**Address** Iera Odos 48 and Megalou Alexandrou 134–136, Kerameikos, Athens 10435, +30 210 3609695 | **Getting there** Metro to Kerameikos (M 3); bus 26, 27, 813, 836, 856, 865 or A 16 | **Hours** Vary according to screenings; check website for schedules (www.tainiothiki.gr) or call ahead | **Tip** The Ideal Cinema (Panepistimiou 46) is the city's oldest working movie theatre. It opened in 1922.

# 41 Grigoropoulos 'Shrine'

*Flowers and graffiti stoke the fire of memory*

On 6 December, 2008, a police officer shot dead a 15-year-old boy – an act that sparked almost a month of rioting in Athens and other Greek cities, and sympathy protests across Europe. The small marble plaque marking the site is often obscured by flowers and poems left by passers-by and its size understates the political passions that the incident ignites even a decade later. Neighbours say not a day goes by without someone placing a flower or small item by the now-chipped marble plaque.

Alexis Grigoropoulos might seem like an unlikely 'revolutionary' hero. The son of a middle-class family, he lived in an affluent suburb and attended private school. But it was the brazen ruthlessness of his death that left most Greeks speechless. Exiting a café in the counter-culture Exarchia district, Grigoropoulos and a small group of friends are said to have taunted two officers from the special police guard – a frequent occurrence in this particular district. Minutes after their verbal altercation ended and the police had driven off, one of the officers returned and shot the boy dead. The news spread rapidly over social media. Within hours the fury had erupted onto the streets of Athens, followed by other cities. Fires literally raged through the weekend as rioters rampaged through the city centre, torching shops and cars; on Monday, school kids spontaneously took to the streets, followed later that week by the unions. It took days to contain the unrest and several more weeks to stamp out the protests.

The riots erupted a year before Greece's government proclaimed the country's plunge into recession – perhaps as a harbinger of the turmoil that lay ahead. It's an incident as potent for the current generation and as much a part of the country's modern history as the Polytechnic students' uprising against the military junta was for their parents 35 years earlier.

Address Corner of Tzavella (also named Alexandrou Grigoropoulou) and Mesolongiou, Exarchia | Getting there Metro to Panepistimio (M 2) or Omonia (M 1 & M 2); bus 21, 22, 25, 26, 27, 54, 60, 100, 224, 230, 608, 622, 732 or 813 | Tip Vinyl never left Exarchia. Music Machine (Didotou 16) has an eclectic LP selection that even drew Lady Gaga.

# 42__Gryllis Water Lilies

*A Marathonian effort to follow a dream*

Every schoolchild learns about the Battle of Marathon and how it changed the course of Western history. Every adult knows about the long-distance race from the bay to the city of Athens that commemorates Pheidippides' (possibly mythical) run to announce the Greeks' victory over the mighty Persians. The area is studded with relics of those days as well as finds from much earlier and the Roman era, but few people suspect that the plain today is a vast market garden.

And most would be surprised to hear that among the ultrafertile vegetable patches and greenhouses there is a water lily nursery with pools and ponds that support 20 different kinds, as well as hundreds of other plants, even some that thrive on air alone.

Curiously, Ioannis Gryllis' love affair with nature began with cactuses at age 12 but books led him to the world of exotic, tropical plants and those are still his favourites. His studies deepened his knowledge and by his early thirties he was growing water lilies on his roof terrace in an Athens suburb. Then he acquired some land near the airport but his plants soon outgrew it, and in 2012, he moved them all – 30 lorries' worth – to a 27,000-square-metre tract in Marathon.

A man with a dream, he has created a nursery for plants of all kinds, organised according to type but also to continent of origin, a personal botanical garden. But the most alluring are the water lily ponds, with their multicoloured flowers, and their multicoloured fish. As Ioannis says, 'I feed the fish and the fish feed the flowers. This water is full of nutrients, the ideal fertiliser.'

Once you've had Ioannis' tour and a taste of his mother's sweets, you may feel up to exploring the historic sites of Marathon: the archaeological museum, the grave tumulus, a 5,000-year-old cemetery, a shrine to Egyptian gods, the start of the famous race, and more. Or you could simply go to the beach.

Address Avlonas 50, Vrana, Marathon, Athens 19007, +30 22940 69534, +30 69777 07208, www.grylliswaterlilies.gr | **Getting there** By car: On Marathon Avenue, follow signs for Archaeological Museum, turn west (Plataion Avenue). Follow signs for Gryllis Water Lilies. In 1.5 km, bear left on Agiou Georgiou and keep going up to where the road forks. Keep right onto Avlonas and you'll come to the nursery. There are little signs most of the way. | **Hours** Daytime, usually open but call to make sure | **Tip** A map showing the location of all the ancient sites in Marathon is posted on the wall of the grave circle shed. Take your pick, or at least visit the (small) museum nearby with sculptures from the villa of Herod Atticus, whose wealth built the theatre below the Acropolis and the first stadium (rebuilt in 1896 for the Olympics).

# 43 __ Guarantee
*Deli sandwiches 'as you like it'*

You may see a queue of people pouring out of this tiny shop onto the street, and wonder what the palpable sense of expectation on their faces is all about. Sans queue to mark the spot, you would no doubt have walked by it without giving it a second glance, so unassuming is its appearance.

Guarantee, which opened in 1988, has glass-enclosed shelves packed with a plethora (130 to be precise) of top-quality deli ingredients, from black truffle salami to pink-centred roast beef, 25 varieties of cheeses from all over Greece and abroad, homemade gravlax salmon, freshly prepared meat or veggie burgers, omelettes and fried eggs and caramelised, marinated or grilled vegetables, as well as chutneys, mustards, spreads and horseradish. The 10 types of bread used are sourced from neighbouring bakeries like nearby Takis, among the best in the city. The sky's the limit not only in the variety of ingredients but in the combinations one can conjure up here. It's all up to how far the customer's imagination, appetite and sandwich know-how can reach. And the perfect accompaniment to their amazing sandwiches is one of their vibrant freshly juiced fruit or vegetable drinks.

Soothingly retro in ambience as well as the warmly familial (yet highly professional), the place is run by a family (Yiannis and Haroula, whose romantic encounter was so intense he impulsively quit the navy and dreamed up creating this business); it was named after the word stamped on Haroula's T-shirt. Although several imitators around the town now boast more polished renditions of the same concept, this is a fast (yet somewhat slow) food place like no other in the capital – and even further afield. Every variety of customer can be found sandwiched in here, with adventurous taste in gourmet foods being the common, near-conspiratorial factor. Indeed, you'll often overhear strangers discussing their personal creations as they wait.

**Address** Veikou 41, Koukaki, Athens 11742, +30 210 9226924, www.toguarantee.gr |
**Getting there** Metro to Syngrou Fix (M2) | **Hours** Mon–Sat 9am–5pm | **Tip**
On 57 Veikou Street is the crumbling former residence of World War II teenage
resistance heroine Iro Konstandopoulou, who underwent three weeks of SS torture
before being executed with 17 bullets, one for each year of her life. All of Koukaki
attended her memorial service as soon as the war ended.

# 44 The Handlebar
*Bicycles, pets and cool customers*

Greece's first cyclists' café was created soon after the opening of a bicycle shop (Vicious Bicycles Athens or VCA) next door, during a time when Athenians left their expensive-to-run cars in the driveway and hopped onto bikes instead. The feel-good factor of getting more exercise, becoming part of a growing community and getting through often congested city traffic at higher speed, while discovering mind-opening side-street shortcuts became a booming antidote. While the bike-shop owners worked on fixing bicycles, customers hung around outside chatting and sipping takeout coffee or a beer on a street ledge, so it made perfect sense to take over an abandoned kafeneion next door and transform it into The Handlebar, a buzzy café-bar that right up to today continues to be an 'institution' for cyclists – and more.

The cosy miniature interior has vintage and rebel touches, with walls that are half lavender paint and half yellow bricks, a minimalist black-tile bar lined with metallic stools and a few tables outside; its warmth comes from the crowds that fill it up. Originally, the lively spot on almost invisible tiny Melanthiou Street had a widely cherished menu centred on indulgent English-style brunches and vegan/vegetarian specials, but today due to financial restraints it serves only smoothies, juices, coffee, Greek herbal teas and plenty of beer, all at very accessible prices.

Its motto is partying and pedalling, and it hosts weekly events such as Punk Wednesday and DJ sets every Friday that crowd the street with dancers. Cyclists gather to plan events (fewer today than in the past as, despite the creation of bike lanes in various parts of Attica, the city is generally too unsafe for cyclists and the trend has dipped significantly) and discuss their hobby, but with its extremely friendly and familial ambience the space welcomes every variety of customer.

Address Melanthiou 8, Psyrri, Athens 10554, +30 211 4093002, www.handlebar.gr |
Getting there Metro to Monastiraki (M1 & M3) | Hours Daily noon–midnight |
Tip Less than 10 minutes' walk away on Karaiskaki Street is The Impact Hub, an ideal
spot to spend the day working in a quiet, communal space and connecting with creative
or business professionals (€10 for the day).

# 45 Hellenic Motor Museum

*Watch out, motor madness can be catching*

When your collection of vintage cars gets out of control and you run out of garage space, it helps to be in the property business. You can simply build a shopping centre and place your Jaguars, Rolls-Royces, Cadillacs, Lancias and Maseratis on the upper floors. Or at least, some of them. Theodore Charagionis, who has won prizes for his shopping malls, owns about 300 vehicles and not even half are on view at this museum.

Yet, the cars on display are works of art, and strolling among them, their owner's obsession is catching. You also feel a wave of admiration for their designers and nostalgia for the automobiles of the last century, as they evolved from boxes on wheels to aerodynamic, sleek speedsters. Each one has its personal story displayed alongside.

The cars are arranged chronologically on three floors, starting with a 1908 Ford Model N and ending with a flock of mostly red Italian sports cars. To get there you can take a lift or ascend a spiral ramp – inspired by New York's Guggenheim – and be entertained by an exhibition on the history of the wheel, with 72 examples, on the way. The museum itself begins with an exact replica of an early auto repair shop with 1930s music to put you in the mood.

As Charagionis tells it, he has been in love with cars since his boyhood, and used to race them, unbeknownst to his parents, until his first child was born in 1977. Then he decided to start restoring them instead. But when building his museum, he also wanted to enhance the location. By surrounding it with a planted courtyard, which induced homeowners to spruce up their façades, and supplying a water feature that actually masks street noise, his Acropole Charagionis received a corporate responsibility award in 2013 for its contribution to society.

Victoria Square may be an unlikely place for rare cars but who would have expected them in Athens in the first place?

Address Triti Septemvriou & Ioulianou 33–35, Victoria Square, Athens 10433, +30 210 8816187, 210 7279999, www.hellenicmotormuseum.gr | Getting there Metro to Victoria Square (M1) and a five-minute walk | Hours Mon–Fri 10am–2pm, Sat & Sun 11am–6pm | Tip Victoria Square is the Athens neighbourhood with the highest refugee population and abounds in ethnic fast food shops, starting with a Georgian bakery across the street from the museum.

# 46 Helmeted Kolokotronis
*The statue 'vandalised' by its sculptor*

Theodoros Kolokotronis is a towering figure in Greek history – a status subliminally suggested by the size and positioning of the bronze statue of the Greek War of Independence general outside the National History Museum. But while visitors often comment on the direction in which Kolokotronis is pointing, few notice the faint inscription on the marble base. Those who do, mistake it for graffiti.

Graffiti it isn't, although it was chiselled into the stone in protest by the statue's sculptor, Lazaros Sohos. The statue is actually a copy, by the same sculptor, of the statue he won a commission in 1884 to make for the town of Nafplio, the Peloponnese port town that served as the Greek capital before its relocation to Athens. Sohos had a slightly different plan for this statue – which like the first was paid for by a national fund-drive. The sculptor wanted to depict Kolokotronis without his helmet. But the commissioning committee disagreed, arguing that the helmet was part of the Old Man of Morea's cherished armour. Sohos complied with their order, but decided to have the last word. Along with his signature, he chiselled a rebuke to the committee on the rear, noting that the helmet had been added 'against his will'. It has taken years for the marks to fade and although no longer legible, they are still visible.

The Kolokotronis statue was first installed at the far corner of the square but moved to its current, more prominent location in 1904. It stands on a bronze pedestal featuring the defeat of Mahmud Dramali Pasha at Dervenakia and Kolokotronis urging Greeks into battle against the Turks. An interesting note: the bronze was cast at a French foundry and exhibited at the 1900 Paris World Fair. It also won a prize, but for the prototype Sohos had created without the helmet, with the general's long, thick hair hanging loose around his shoulders.

**Address** Plateia Kolokotroni, Athens 10561 | **Getting there** Metro to Syntagma (M2 & M3); bus 1, 2, 4, 5, 11, 12, 15, 25, 26 or 27 | **Tip** Check the inscription on the base of the nearby bust of Harilaos Trikoupis, seven-time premier in the late 19th century. It reads what could be a national motto: 'Greece wants to live and it will live'.

# 47 The Hidden Arch Bridge

*Walk along the exposed banks of an ancient river*

Every day thousands of Athenians driving into or from the city centre cross an overpass that few know exists. Built in the mid-1850s, the concrete and stone arch bridge supports the section of the asphalt where Leoforos Vouliagmenis segues into Athanasiou Diakou at the south-western corner of the site of the Temple of Zeus. The bridge straddles the banks of the only exposed section of the Ilissos, a river that marked a boundary of ancient Athens and that is now covered by the modern city.

Most of the bridge has been engulfed by the concrete used to build the road above, but one section on the north side has been preserved. The southern side has been closed, but it's worth exploring the exposed section. Walking along the temple side of the street, you'll notice a low wall just before the tram tracks. Peer over the side for a glimpse of the dry river bed below, then follow the steps off Ardittou down to the church of Agia Foteini – a small, 4th century basilica built over a temple dedicated to Hecate. A footpath at the far end of the paved courtyard circles back to the bridge, whose supports and arch are now visible through the foliage. The riverbed is dry, but can be slippery after rain. For a second, it's easy to imagine that the muffled sputtering of motorbikes overhead is the croaking of the frogs that once populated the area and gave the neighbourhood its name, *Vatrahonisi* or frog island.

The bridge was completed during the reign of Otto I, 'King of Greece', according to the dedication chiselled into the girder masonry. The Bavarian prince who was installed as Greece's first king in 1832 is the only monarch to bear that title – his successors were all known as 'King of the Hellenes'. The site may have some metaphysical link to the ending of reigns: by some accounts, Kodros, the last king of ancient Athens, is buried there too. Its urban myth among treasure-hunters that a piece of gold he was carrying is wedged somewhere in the soil.

Address Corner of Kalirrois and Vouliagmenis | Getting there Metro to Syngrou-Fix (M 2); tram; bus 2, 4, 10, 11, 165, 227, 550, 856 or A 3 | Tip The shallow cave in the rock behind the church was likely dedicated to the worship of the god Pan.

# 48 Junta Resistance Museum
*An ancient sanctuary for modern-day pagans*

The cluster of tree-shaded cottages at the far end of Eleftherias Park is unusually pastoral and, once you realise what took place in these quaint-looking buildings, disturbingly central. The compound (not surprisingly, originally the infantry barracks) is the former detention centre of the Greek Military Police, or ESA, and its notorious Special Investigative Section, or EAT, where anti-junta activists were interrogated – a process that mostly employed torture. And the museum is a small, if not obscure, monument to that period and its aftermath, the *metapolitefsi*, which has left a less pronounced but perhaps deeper mark on the country than the civil war that followed Greece's liberation from the Nazis.

Indeed, the fall of the seven-year military dictatorship that began on 21 April, 1967 with a coup by a group of ultra-nationalist far-right colonels is usually commemorated in the annual march on 17 November from the Polytechnic, near the National Archaeological Museum, to the American Embassy on the area adjacent to Eleftherias Park. The student uprising precipitated the junta's collapse the following July, but it was the resistance of individuals or groups tortured at EAT-ESA that stoked the dissidence. Some, like Alekos Panagoulis, gained global fame. But most faded back into the ordinariness of their daily lives that poignantly intersects with some of the exhibits – a photograph, a letter. Save for these items, the interior has been left virtually intact. The peeling paint and rusted window bars make the stories of those who were incarcerated and tortured here uncomfortably real. More so when members of the Association of Prisoners and Exiled Resistance Fighters that created and maintains this museum briefly reenact their experiences here. It is a memory that still causes pain, but for those who bled here, not remembering is more painful. It is a message underscored by the German organisers' decision to open Documenta14 here.

Address Parko Eleftherias, Athens 11521, +30 210 7258258 | Getting there Metro to Megaro Moussikis (M 3); bus 3, 10, 22, 60, 550 or A 5 | Hours Irregular, but accommodating for visitors; phone first | Tip A small group of stone shelters with wooden hip roofs at the far end of the park, bordering Deinokratous Street, housed Greece's first military hospital in 1904 and are being restored for use as a library and cultural centre.

# 49  Kaisariani Monastery Gardens

*An organised wilderness on Hymettus*

Hymettus, the fabled violet-hued mountain to the east of Athens, looks thickly wooded now but in 1945 there was nothing left of the forest but stubs. Starving Athenians had felled all the trees to keep warm during the bitter winters of the Nazi occupation. In that year, Katy Argyropoulou, president of the Friends of the Trees (*Philodas-siki*), an organisation founded in 1899, embarked on a programme of reforestation. Within a decade, they had planted three million trees over 600 hectares, and had also undertaken to restore the abandoned 11th-century monastery on the mountain's lower slopes.

The monastery, dedicated to the Virgin but built over the ruins of a temple to Aphrodite, is now a model of Byzantine architecture. It stands in an area of three springs, one of which provided much of Athens' water supply before the construction of the Marathon dam in 1929.

By the 1960s, the Friends created a botanical garden next to the monastery. Since then, with 400 species of plants mostly from Crete and the Peloponnese, plus a few pre-existing 'aliens' from Australia and Lebanon, it has won several awards and is one of the European Union's Historic Gardens.

Some of the more insignificant-looking shrubs might only be of interest to botanists, but this horseshoe-shaped garden arranged on the steep slopes of a ravine is a delight in all seasons. It's a labour of love since weeding in winter and watering in summer are done only by hand, with the plants otherwise left to their own devices. As the curator says, 'Plants are neurotic, they grow only where they want to.' So this is a natural botanical garden, very unlike the orderly ones you may be used to.

Its serene atmosphere and magnificent views offer a refuge to city-weary Athenians and visitors.

Address Kaisariani Monastery, Mount Hymettus, Attica 16122, +30 210 7220866, 210 7231769, www.philodassiki.org | Getting there Bus 223 or 224 from Kanningos Square to upper Kaisariani district and then 30 minutes' walk or taxi | Hours Mon – Sat 8.30am – 1.30pm; no charge, donations welcome. Guided tours for two or more by appointment. Aesthetic Garden never closed for walks. | Tip The Botanical Garden also runs an on-site nursery with 120 Greek plants only, raised without chemicals or fertilisers.

# 50 Kallidromiou Market
*Ultra-fresh produce and not an anarchist in sight*

Athens is said to boast 44 street markets, but that's an old figure. Each of its neighbourhoods hosts one every week and many also welcome organic markets. On those days, traffic is disrupted, parking's even more impossible, and yet the farmers' or 'people's' market (*laiki agora*) is a beloved institution that will be celebrating its 90th anniversary in 2019. They were the brainchild of Venizelos, during his final term as prime minister (1928–1932). And they support small farmers as well as giving city dwellers direct access to the freshest fruit and veg at low prices.

Even if you don't wish to shop, a walk on a street lined with the best Greek produce is a feast for all the senses. You'll be overwhelmed by the sheer bounty – there's no sign of a crisis here. Ebony aubergines, shiny tomatoes, enormous pumpkins, pyramids of potatoes, aromatic strawberries, glistening greens and lettuces, some sold by the growers themselves, some by professional vendors supplied by wholesalers, crowd the stalls, all varying with the seasons. But you'll also find fish, honey, nuts and bins of olives, waiting to be sampled, as well as dried herbs, cut flowers and potted plants, bags of pulses, household goods and even racy red lingerie. Bury your nose in a bunch of oregano, try to resist the scent of grilling souvlaki.

These are social occasions too, as regulars chat with the vendors and as neighbour meets neighbour. But we recommend the Kallidromiou market since it stretches across Exarchia and provides a different glimpse of that notorious hotbed of anarchists.

Here you will see utterly average people of all ages against a background of graffiti-splattered walls, elegant town houses, ruined buildings, tree-lined steps and a banner proclaiming Asteras 1928, a sports club.

And you need fear no riots or protest marches, though you may well be given a flyer announcing one in the near future.

Address Kallidromiou, from Kountourioti to Harilaou Trikoupi, Exarchia 10683 | Getting there Metro to Omonia (M 2 & M 3), and walk up Themistokleous or take bus 230, 025 or 026 from Panepistimiou | Hours Sat 8am–2/3pm | Tip The Ama Lahei restaurant in an old schoolhouse with courtyard at number 69 is a great place for lunch (opens at 1pm) or dinner (+30 210 3845978).

# 51 Kallirhoe Parren

*Greece's forgotten suffragette*

The Athens First Cemetery has been declared a museum – and rightfully so, as a tour of its graves is like a walk through modern Greek history since most of the country's leading political and cultural figures are buried here. For this reason, it's often included in guides to the city, which usually point visitors to sculptor Yannoulis Halepas' *Sleeping Maiden*, a memorial to an 18-year-old girl who died of tuberculosis. Oddly, there's nary a mention of Kallirhoe Parren, the woman at her bedside when she died and whose grave is a few metres away. It's an interesting oversight as Parren is a formidable figure (although the bust itself is unremarkable).

Born in 1861 in Rethymno, Crete, she was raised in Athens after her family relocated when she was six. She graduated from the French school, studied to be a teacher and taught briefly at a school in Odessa. But it was after she returned to Greece that she made her mark, as a journalist and publisher of one of Greece's first newspapers for women. Her career was no doubt encouraged by her husband, Ioannis Parren, a Greek from Constantinople with a French and British background who founded the state-run Athens News Agency. Through her weekly paper, *Efimeris ton Kyrion* (*Ladies' Journal*), which was run entirely by women, Parren campaigned for extending public education and voting rights to women. Returning from a women's conference in Chicago in 1893, she founded the Union for the Emancipation of Women, which paved the way for Greece's suffragette movement. In 1917, her politics landed her in exile for six months.

Parren died in 1940, 12 years before women were given the right to vote and run for office. Her work has been posthumously recognised, although she is mostly praised for her extensive contributions to charity and culture, especially through the founding of the Greek Women's Lyceum.

**Address** Logginou 2 and Anapafseos, Athens 11636, +30 210 9221621 | **Getting there** Train to Zappio or Leotoros Vouliagmenis; bus 2, 4, 10, 11, 165, 227, 550, 790, 856 or A3 | **Hours** Daily, sunrise to sunset | **Tip** Preparatory rituals for the Eleusinian Mysteries were held at the Temple of Artemis Agroterra, an open excavation at Ardittou 24.

# 52 Kapnikareas Café

*Where you can eat to the beat of Greek blues*

Rebetika music, whose tinkling bouzouki and raspy voices are as much a part of Greece as a seaside taverna, has often been compared to American blues. They both had their origins in the urban underworld, whether the Black slums of the Deep South or the hash dens and sleazy ports of Piraeus and Thessaloniki, in the early 20th century. Their lyrics are full of woe, lost love, desperation, drugs and bravado, but even if you don't understand them, the sounds will always remind you of Greece.

Usually to listen to this music you have to wait till near midnight, but at this café, rebetika starts playing around lunchtime, ending at 11pm. No signs alert you to this cheerful dive, tucked into an alley close to the Byzantine church it's named after, so follow your ears.

It had its start in 1977, when Sotiris Sofos, a tailor, decided to shift careers and opened a sandwich shop, an innovation back then. Twenty years later, his son, Dimitris, abandoned his job as a sound engineer at TV and radio stations to follow his two hobbies, music and food. He broadened the menu – cooking many dishes himself, inspired by his travels to India and the Middle East – and invited his musician friends to drop by.

Every day different people show up, from as many as 20 groups, duos and larger. They may play 'island' style, 'swing' and even rockabilly with rebetika, a far cry from the controversial, explicit songs that were censored, even banned by Greek dictatorships before and after the war.

The blue-walled interior incorporates instruments in its décor, along with old photos and octagonal Indian lamps with a reddish glow. The menu features lots of mezedes as well as main courses, so you can eat 'on a shoestring', as Dimitris says, aware of Greeks' empty-wallet syndrome. But do try his grandma's meatballs from Ikaria, the island where people forget to die. She's 100 and still going strong.

**Address** Christopoulou 2 & Ermou 57, Athens 10563, +30 210 3227394 | Getting there Metro to Monastiraki (M1 & M3) or Syntagma (M2 & M3), and a 10-minute walk | Hours Daily early morning–11pm, music starts around 2pm | Tip Kapnikareas church, one of the city's oldest, was built in the mid-11th century on the foundations of a temple of Athena or Demeter, but the wall paintings inside are by a modern master, Fotis Kontoglou, in 1955.

# 53 Katakouzenos Apartment

*A multi-layered love story in a literary salon*

They were well-born and beautiful, but they were also cultivated, idealists, patriots and polyglots. Angelos Katakouzenos was a French-trained psychiatrist and intellectual. His wife Leto wrote the first play by a woman to be performed at the National Theatre, as well as novels and short stories. Their circle of friends transcended Athens and included Camus, Faulkner, Chagall and Hubert Humphrey, in addition to almost every Greek artist and poet of the time (from the 1930s to 1980s).

A visit to their apartment is a trip back to that golden era, when ideas and principles seemed more important than fame and riches. But don't think of it as a museum in the normal sense but rather as an invitation to step inside an exceptional private home. With the hosts temporarily absent, you can poke around their belongings and puzzle out their personalities. Chagall's portrait of Leto, Picasso's drawings, Ghika's remarkable 'four-seasons' doors, Tsarouchis' paintings were all gifts, not purchases, as were the objects and signed books. Even the furniture has a story and the place exudes light and love.

Curator Sophia Peloponnisiou compares the apartment to Orhan Pamuk's Museum of Innocence in Istanbul, but 'that was fiction, the objects acquired to tell a love story he invented. While this was real.'

Discovering Leto's book about her husband when she was 19, Sophia fell in love herself with the couple's integrity and values and became close to Leto, who survived Angelos by 15 years and created a foundation to preserve the house and enable it to live again after her death in 1997. Imagine Sophia's surprise when Leto's will named her as curator. Since 2008, the Katakouzenos House Museum has offered lectures, concerts, exhibitions and performances that keep its owners' literary salon and their spirit alive. Running it is a labour of love, too, as its staff are all volunteers.

Address Amalias 4, 5th floor, Syntagma, Athens 10557, +30 694 4825164, www.katakouzenos.gr | Getting there Metro to Syntagma (M2 & M3) and two minutes' walk | Hours After 5pm, by appointment | Tip It's worth a visit if only for the amazing view of the National Gardens and Parliament exactly opposite.

# 54 Klimataria

*For whoever is lonely there is Klimataria*

It is unlikely that the Austrian poet Georg Trakl had Klimataria in mind when he wrote that 'for whoever is lonely there is a tavern', but it is the perfect description for a place as known for its *parea* as it is for its food and wine. You'll see few couples dining here – and those at smaller tables are often joined with larger groups by the evening's end.

Located in the heart of the city's 'historical centre', Klimataria has occupied the same site since 1927 when an enterprising parishioner converted it from a church coffee house to an *oenomageireio* to serve the cordwainers in the district's leather workshops. It has since resisted the waves of gentrification that have washed through the market district. Even after being gutted by fire in 2005, the owners turned down development offers. Instead, they rebuilt the cottage-style structure with its walled courtyard, replaced the wine barrels lining the walls, and hired an artist to recreate the old signage and décor.

True to its roots as an *oenomageireio* – a distinct category of cheap taverna that served workmen coming off early shifts a small tin carafe of wine (oenos) and a plate of hot food – Klimataria's menu is built around *mageirefta*. Simple, familiar recipes, they invoke the warmth of home. Cooked slowly in a clay pot or *gastra*, they produce a thick sauce, which is perfect for mopping up with Klimataria's freshly baked bread and savouring slowly between sips of wine.

Klimataria has its regulars; maybe not daily patrons as in the 1920s and 1930s, but even today many diners find themselves running into old friends or acquaintances. In the old days, a patron might pick up a *baglamas* to play; today, musicians who play on weekends are professionals but it's not uncommon for one or more of the owners to pick up an instrument to strum on nights when the wine and feeling of *parea* flow.

Address Plateia Theatrou 2, Athens 10552, +30 210 3216629 | Getting there Metro to Omonia (M1 & M2) or Monastiraki (M1 & M3) | Hours Daily noon–2am | Tip Live Greek music on Saturday night. Be sure to book ahead! Like backgammon? The Diplareios Crafts School (+30 210 3240130) a few doors along, offers one-day marquetry classes where you can make your own boards.

# 55 Kokotos Winery

*Sacred to Dionysos and St George the Intoxicator*

The story starts in 1975 when George and Anne Kokotos bought a 10-acre clearing in the middle of a forest in the municipality of Dionysos, named after the wine god, on the north slopes of Mount Pendeli. Raised in a wine-growing district of Crete, George had a nostalgic vision of making his own, while Anne, unusually for the time, grew up in a wine-loving family in the UK.

When they planted their first vines in 1980, the Greek wine revolution had yet to occur. People drank mostly retsina, filling their demijohns from barrels in moonshiners' basements, with no quality controls. Bottled wines were a rarity. But with entry into the EEC (now EU), came an economic boom, subsidies, courses in oenology, new methods of cultivating and vinification, and the Greek wine industry took off. The first vines planted here and elsewhere tended to be international – Chardonnay, Cabernet Sauvignon, Merlot – more prestigious than the Savvatiano used for retsina. But with time, more and more native varieties are being discovered and resuscitated, some winning lavish praise from critics.

Since then George and Anne have added more varieties, all organically grown, pressed in their modern facilities and aged in oak and acacia barrels before bottling. As this is their home, visitors receive a more personal welcome and tour than at a larger vineyard. The views alone are worth the trip. Two disastrous fires burned the surrounding forest in 1990 and 2009, but they miraculously spared the property and now you can taste their seven wines with a 360-degree panorama of the mountains of Attica and the Aegean below.

As for St George, the dragon slayer has two feast days, in April and 3 November, when vintners traditionally open their barrels to taste the new wine. He thus acquired the epithet Intoxicator and the estate includes a chapel dedicated to him, where the inebriated can find solace.

Address Stamata, Attica 14575, +30 210 8145113, +30 6946 068010, +30 6948 509580, www.ktimakokotou.gr | Getting there Bus 509 to Stamata Square (and pick up from winery); train from Larissa Station to Agios Stephanos and taxi | Hours Open house first Sunday of every month, 11am–4pm; tours by appointment only | Tip Visit their daughter Natalie Kokotou's permaculture/biodynamic vegetable garden next door, a now thriving piece of land where nothing would grow, with rabbits, chickens and two ponies.

# 56 Ktima Aristi

*Living an organic country life in the city*

A century ago, suburbs like Kifissia and Halandri were not part of the Athens urban landscape but considered to be part of the countryside. Ktima Aristi recreates that pastoral scene in a farm that fuses agricultural tradition with the needs of contemporary lifestyles – something its founders have dubbed 'a cultured life'. It's not just food but about literally cultivating our link to the environment.

Ktima Aristi was launched in 2017 by Aristi Sarra. The estate's name is derived from its founder's but also echoes the Greek word for excellent or perfect, *arista*. And the experience at the one-and-a-quarter-acre landscaped farm with blockstone walks and perfectly aligned vegetable rows is certainly a perfect escape from everyday city life. Inspiration for this urban country estate came from Sarra's experiences that include culinary studies in London and later San Francisco. This was all distilled into the design of Ktima Aristi on an abandoned lot that somehow escaped developers' rapacious appetite for land in this popular suburb just minutes by metro from the centre of Athens. It is a relaxing space; not a fairy-tale farm but a place where you can imagine living – and where you'd like to.

The concept behind Ktima Aristi isn't farm to table but rather table to farm. Products from the farm are sold at the general store located in a small cottage shaded by a massive tree. The tree's cover extends to a covered terrace with picnic tables and benches where visitors can rest with a refreshment from the small café. Visitors are also welcome to picnic anywhere in the grounds. Art shows, a summer camp, seminars and workshops as diverse as cooking classes for children, planting an urban vegetable garden, meditation, storytelling and the properties of medicinal herbs are regularly organised in a sheltered space or, in mild weather, outdoors. Hardly surprisingly, Ktima Aristi is popular among families with children, either as a day out or for hosting parties.

Address Ploutarchou and Keas, Halandri 15234, +30 210 6085559 | Getting there
Metro to Agia Paraskevi (M3) or Chalandri (M3); bus 1 or 404 | Hours Wed–Fri
10am–5pm, Sat & Sun 10am–4pm | Tip Rema Halandriou ('Halandri stream') is a
protected park with stone footbridges and a summer theatre.

# 57__Ktistakis

*Doughnut 'holes' and nothing else since 1912*

Once upon a time, a young man left his native Crete to seek his fortune in Alexandria. While there, he worked in a sweetshop where he made *loukoumades*, Greek doughnuts, a word rooted in the Persian *lokma*, meaning 'bite'. Returning to Chania in 1912, he set up his own business, and his family has kept it going ever since. When he died in 1955, his three sons moved to Athens and opened their own shop near the National Theatre off Omonia Square. In 1997, they moved to their present location around the corner.

With its brown bentwood chairs, marble tables and tile floor, the small room looks much older. Half of the shop is the kitchen, where Thodoris, named after his grandfather and now 46, has been frying bite-sized balls of batter since he was 18. 'My father died on a Wednesday, and by Monday I was on the job.'

Remarkably, the Ktistakis family has never made anything else. But if you have the recipe for perfection, why change? Athens boasts several *loukoumades* places, some traditional – deep-fried batter rings or knobs, drizzled with honey syrup – some modern, stuffed with chocolate or flavoured custards. But these 'Chania-type' bites are different. Smaller, they come sprinkled with cinnamon and sesame seeds, while the syrup lurks inside, a burst of sweetness as they enter your mouth.

How does it get there? Not by injection, as some customers have speculated. It's a secret. Another difference is that the dough (flour, water, sugar, a little yeast and cinnamon and some dough from the previous batch) is made the night before, left to rest, and then the balls are fried, to be refried on order. It doesn't sound like much, except that people come from all over the city to get their fix. It's a sweet one doesn't outgrow.

As for Thodoris, he would never leave the centre. 'Omonia is the real Athens, I love it, and right now, it's the immigrants who hold it together.'

Address Sokratous 59, Omonia, Athens 10431, +30 210 5240891 | Getting there Metro to Omonia (M2 & M3), and a five-minute walk | Hours Mon–Fri 9am–8pm, Sat 10am–8pm, Sun 11am–8pm; closed on Sundays in summer | Tip The National Theatre opened in 1900 as the Royal Theatre and was designed by Ernst Ziller, the celebrity architect of the period. Pop round after a bite and take in a show or see an exhibition.

# 58 Kypseli
*The doggiest neighbourhood in Athens*

Statues or busts of heroes or politicians adorn many Athens squares. Kypseli, a district with no must-see landmarks, has them too. But it also boasts the capital's only statue of a dog. A hunting hound, he sits regally in the park that runs down the centre of its main street.

Although legends abound regarding this dignified pooch – that he saved a child who fell into the river now covered by the street or was drowned himself after rescuing his master – none of them is true. The sculptor, Euripides Vavouris, simply loved animals and placed his masterpiece here in 1940, a few years after the river was turned into a 'Green Avenue'.

In those days, Upper Kypseli was being transformed from countryside into an aristocratic residential area with smart Bauhaus-inspired apartment buildings, some of which survived the post-war construction orgy that turned it into the district with the highest population density in Athens. But the river had become a bog and a health hazard.

Instead of cementing it over, the city fathers had trees and bushes planted along and in it, creating fountains, pools and rivulets where ducks used to swim. Today, not quite as watery, the Green Avenue is a long wide oasis and Fokionos Negri Street has been pedestrianised. Or perhaps, 'caninised'.

Here you will see dogs of all kinds and sizes from Chihuahuas to Great Danes, Hungarian Pumis and, of course mongrels, as well as strays. An unspoken hierarchy exists: big dogs gather with younger owners at the top of the street; little old dogs with little old ladies (and gents) sit on benches in the centre; middle-sized dogs walk with middle-aged owners below them. The Green Avenue is people-friendly too; kids of all colours play football here and older men play dominos on the edges of the square, while cafés, bars and tavernas on both sides of the avenue buzz night and day like bees in this hive.

Address Fokionos Negri, Kypseli, Athens 11257 | Getting there Bus 022 or 622; trolley 2 and 4 or walk from Viktoria Metro station | Tip For an area with so many dogs, it's a tribute to their owners that Fokionos Negri is 'poo free'!

# 59 Lake Vouliagmeni

*Curative springs and mysterious phenomena*

Underwater nymphs who lure divers to their death, doctor fish that nip at your skin, the largest underwater cave in the world and curative thermal waters that have eased people of their ailments for over 2,000 years are all part of the truth and mythology of Lake Vouliagmeni. Located to the south of Athens on the south-west foot of the Hymettus mountain range and across from Vouliagmeni beach, the lake's brackish waters are said to be especially beneficial for those suffering from skin or gynaecological problems, as well as rheumatism and arthritis, because of the high mineral content (calcium, potassium, iodine, sodium and a minor level of radiation).

Once a giant cavern that collapsed following an earthquake, the lake has four large caves that have been explored 20 times throughout the decades by Greek and foreign expert and amateur divers attempting to map them. In separate instances, eight divers lost their lives during their explorations in the labyrinthine underworld, and legend has it that they were trapped by the 'haunted' lake's fairies or nymphs, although experts maintain that the accidents were due to faulty equipment or lack of experience. There are 14 underground tunnels around the lake, including the world's largest, which is 800 metres in length, 80 metres deep and 60–150 metres wide.

Once free to all visitors and especially popular among the elderly locals who came year-round to swim in its warm (23–29°C) waters, under private ownership it has acquired an entry fee and a somewhat more glamorous vibe. The emerald green lake, made up of fresh spring and sea water, is surrounded by rock walls and lush greenery, and with the sunloungers, umbrellas and good quality bar-restaurant can easily lure one to spend several hours there dipping in and out, while some come especially to be nibbled on by *Garra rufa*, aka 'doctor fish'.

Address Vouliagmeni Lake, Vouliagmeni 16671, +30 210 8962237, www.limnivouliagmenis.gr | Getting there Bus 122 from Metro Elliniko, bus 115, 116 or 117 from Glyfada | Hours Daily 8am–5.30pm | Tip If you head to the lively Astir coastline nearby, visit the 6th-century B.C. Temple of Apollo Zoster at the back of the beach.

# 60 Lela Karagianni House

*Wartime resistance headquarters preserved as tech hub*

From outside, the two-storey townhouse – home to a local pharmacist, his wife and their seven children – looked like any other residence in this middle-class neighbourhood. But from inside, 43-year-old Lela Karagianni ran an espionage operation against the Nazis and organised the escape from Greece of some 150 British officers after German troops occupied the city. Code-named 'Bouboulina' after the heroine of Greece's War of Independence from the Ottoman Turks, the spy network stole material about German ship movements and collected information that helped the resistance identify Nazi collaborators. Its history as a data centre of sorts makes it somehow fitting that the building is temporarily being used as an information technology training hub by Microsoft, which donated €150,000 towards its restoration.

Karagianni's story is compelling. She not only funded the network herself, but recruited her husband and five of their children into it. Early on, her activity drew the authorities' attention and she was arrested in October 1941. But she resumed her covert action after her release a few months later. In 1944, a double-agent operation fell apart; she was arrested with two associates and taken to a prison camp on the city's outskirts where she was executed that September with other resistance members. Despite some controversy over that final operation's failure, she has been posthumously honoured by the Academy of Athens and recognised by Yad Vashem as Righteous Among Nations for helping Greek Jews.

Renovated and opened to the public in late 2017, the Karagianni house will likely be converted to a community centre after the period for which its use has been ceded to the tech company expires. Neighbourhood associations and other groups have submitted proposals for a library, a local history museum, and, yes, a job training centre.

Address Lelas Karagianni 1 and Stavropoulou, Kypseli, Athens 11252 | Getting there Bus 3, 5, 11, 14, 54, 608 or A 8 | Tip When visiting the National Archaeological Museum, look for a marble bust of Lela Karagianni on the Tositsa pedestrian walk.

# 61 Limba
*A smashing time in Athens*

By now there are a multitude of bars and clubs where you can get wrecked in Athens, but until recently there has been no establishment where you are welcomed to go on a rampage, and then walk away as if it never happened. Limba, a basement business in the heart of Monastiraki, is a modern-day allegory for the pent-up exasperation that Greeks have amassed during a long period of biting financial crises, alarming regional wars and terrorism, bad presidents and jaded love. It exemplifies a deep-seated compulsion for that furore to be released, ironically in a private, organised, financially viable way. For some it is simply an atypical destination for a lark.

Upon arriving, the client peruses a menu to satiate a seething, or otherwise just whimsical disastrous intent. Starting with prices from a handful of euros and reaching to over 100, the menu choices are set by how many out-of-order objects / symbolic technological victims one may opt to smash to smithereens. They include old computer monitors, mobile phones, TV screens, bottles and crockery. After selecting a 'package', the client is asked to don a protective body suit complete with helmet, visor and a double layer of gloves.

There are two soundproof rooms to choose from, both painted in a deliberately uncouth way to resemble either a living room or a DIY workshop, and in each, a selection of weapons of mass destruction, such as baseball bats and iron rods, are laid out. Limba's manager offers the client two luxuries – the choice of music (classical and traditional Greek are the most popular by far), and the freedom to take as long as necessary. Regulars here fit the mould of life-crisis-angst stereotypes: middle-aged business persons, 30-year-old women, teenagers and tourists just out for a laugh. The owners are ecologists, and make sure to recycle every single remaining fragment after each booking. You could say that they recycle everything twice - the first time by making broken, useless objects ideal for breaking breakable.

Address Pittaki 6, Psyrri, Athens 10554, +30 698 1373351 | Getting there Metro or HSAP Electric Railway to Monastiraki (M1 & M3) | Hours Tue–Sun 5–10pm | Tip Monastiraki is a hub of social, gastronomical and cultural activity, including the Flea Market, the Athens Cathedral and the city's best souvlaki joints. Combine your Limba visit with a drink, food and tour.

# 62 Lover's Leap
*Athens' own real-life 'Romeo and Juliet'*

The Parthenon's friezes provide enough drama – both artistic in their content and real-life in Greece's legal battle with the British Museum for their return – by themselves. But few visitors are aware of the drama they've provided to Athenian society: an incident in the city's history that is memorialised in the local colloquialism, 'I will leap off the Acropolis' as a hyperbolic (sometimes mocking) response to shocking news.

The phrase, used only by Athenians, harks back to the late 19th century and star-crossed love of a real-life Romeo and Juliet. 'Romeo' was the army doctor Michalis Mimikos and 'Juliet' was the German palace governess Mary Weber. They had fallen madly in love after meeting in the palace gardens, where they continued meeting in secret. Romance took a turn towards tragedy when Mary's father refused to bless their marriage. The desperate young woman wrote to her beau, saying they had to be wed to save her honour as their affair was now public. Heartbroken when several letters to Michalis went unanswered, she climbed to the highest point she knew – the peak of the Parthenon frieze – and, on a moonlit night, flung herself off the sacred hill.

But it was all a misunderstanding. The young doctor had failed to receive the letters, which were sent to the hospital, because he had been in bed with a fever for a week. Learning of Mary's death – described in great detail by an oddly passive guard who didn't seem to make any effort to stop her – the grief-stricken young man shot himself with a service revolver. The double suicide stunned Athenian society. Thanks to friends, they were later reburied together in a joint grave at the Athens First Cemetery. The tale of their star-crossed romance was memorialised in a 1958 film, several popular songs, and, in the incident's immediate aftermath, in a spate of suicides and suicide threats.

Address Acropolis Hill, Athens 11742, +30 210 3214172 | Getting there Metro to Acropolis (M2) | Hours Daily, summer 8am–7.30pm, winter 8.30am–3pm | Tip The Temple of Asclepius, accessed from Dionysiou Areopagitou, leads very close to the rocks where Mary was found.

# 63 Lower Ermou Street

*A street art gallery without an inch of blank wall*

You can see street art, tags, stencils and scribbles, ranging from brilliant masterpieces to mindless vandalism, all over the city. But there are few places where graffiti cover such a long stretch with such variety. This cobbled, carless section of Ermou connects the Thissio metro / train station area with the former Gas Works entertainment centre. The promenade passes the length of Kerameikos, Athens' ancient cemetery, all green and marble, should your eyes tire of bright colours and phantasmagorical shapes and patterns.

This could be the moment to think about graffiti, an age-old tradition harking back to the time when athletes incised comments on walls near stadiums. And a reminder that the word comes from the Greek *grapho*, which initially meant to carve or engrave, and now means to write.

Credit for the first recorded modern tag, Taki183, also goes to a young Greek, in 1969 in New York. Thousands everywhere copied his 'cool' initiative and it blossomed into an art form. You can argue that it's not always art, not always appropriate or welcome, but on Ermou, there are dozens of examples.

At the Gazi end, famous artists and crews were commissioned to paint the warehouse walls. Here you can see giant murals by Raven, Sive (an art teacher from Volos whose caricatures appear in *The New Yorker*), and across Pireos Street on the Gas Works walls by INO and AIVA, who always work together.

Things to note: a halo means the artist has died; the best artists are called kings (INO crowned himself); one paints nothing but 'happy penises'; a (master)piece deserves respect and is not meant to be tagged or scribbled over. But street art is nothing if not ephemeral, and it's intended to make you think. Some of these surreal, scary, distorted figures may give you nightmares but they won't leave you unmoved. They are proof that creativity flourishes in unsettled times.

Address Lower Ermou, from Thissio to Pireos, Athens 10553 | Getting there Metro to Thissio (M1), and a two-minute walk to the start | Tip The Kerameikos is named after the potters, think ceramists, who lived there, close to the clay on the banks of the Eridanos River and on the edge of the cemetery. They were kept busy making funerary urns and tomb ornaments.

# 64__Lyceum Club
## of Greek Women
*Souvenirs of folk traditions*

The ankle-height vitrine in a 1920s townhouse on a Kolonaki side street is easy to miss, but if you're looking for authentic or even one-of-a-kind souvenirs, this boutique museum shop run by the Lyceum Club of Greek Women is the place to go. Founded by Kalliope Parren in 1911 to promote women and volunteerism, the Greek Women's Lyceum grounded its mission in preserving tradition. Today it's the preeminent authority on Greek dance and costume, with several regional dance troupes that offer classes and perform in Greece and abroad. And if you've been lulled into thinking that Greek dance is exhausted by Zorba's heel-slapping *Opa!*s (the syrtaki, by the way, didn't exist before the film), a quick tour of the charming collection in the Lyceum headquarters above the shop is a revelation.

Dress has been an important element of Greek culture since antiquity and, along with food, reflects differences between regions – not just geographic, but social too. The Lyceum's collection is like a panorama of Greek folk traditions, with the designs and accessories signalling social but also personal information, like the wearer's natal village and marital status. Even how a scarf is tied or if it's worn around the shoulders or waist is significant.

The motifs from the costumes are replicated on items, mostly handmade, for sale in the Lyceum Club's little shop. Mementoes range from the familiar – T-shirts, coffee mugs, wall calendars, cloth shopping bags – to the off-beat or eclectic, like the snug velvet *kontogouni* bodice or tasselled caps with plaited gold threads. The ceramics are hand-thrown and almost everything is knitted, embroidered or woven by Lyceum craft circles around Greece – or even at the looms in the rear where you can watch skilled weavers transform strands of wool into gorgeous tapestries, often to custom-ordered designs.

**Address** Dimokritou 7A, Kolonaki, Athens 10673, +30 210 3611607 | **Getting there** Metro to Syntagma (M2 & M3) | **Hours** Mon–Fri 10am–2pm | **Tip** Pick up a box of marrons déguisés – chestnuts covered in milk or dark chocolate – from Desire Patisserie across the street.

# 65 — The Maid of Athens

*Mystery surrounds the girl in Byron's poem*

'Maid of Athens, ere we part / Give, oh give back my heart', the opening lines to Lord Byron's oft-cited poem 'Maid of Athens', unequivocally declare his infatuation with the unnamed young woman. While this beauty's identity was never really a secret, there is a minor, more localised controversy over where she lived.

Byron's 'maid' was none other than Teresa Makri, the young daughter (by some accounts, a scandalously young 12 years old) of the widow with whom the poet briefly took lodging. Makri grew up to be a celebrated beauty, 'a Caryatis come to life' according to one description, and married a British officer, sadly dying in poverty in 1875.

Makri's identity was briefly in question as Byron expressed his infatuation with all three of the widow's daughters. However, there is a slight disagreement over the location of the house in which Byron first met her in 1797 and again during separate stays in 1809 as well as February and July 1810. By most accounts, that address is given as Number 14 Agias Theklas – but sadly the building that stood there collapsed in the 1970s after being abandoned for decades. The lot is still empty today, presumably earning more for its owners as a car park than it would as a rental property. But not everyone agrees that this is where the Makri family lived. A drawing, purportedly of their home, shows it standing on a corner, which would place it a few metres from the 'official' spot. The two-storey dwelling in the illustration also looks shorter than the building that occupied the lot at Number 14. Others dismiss the claim, saying it's just an attempt to raise that property's value. Regardless, there is no doubt that the Makri family lived on that block.

Teresa was christened in Agia Eleousa, which has since been engulfed by the Criminal Court at Number 4 Agias Theklas; her father is also buried there.

Address Agias Theklas 14, Psyrri, Athens 10554 | Getting there Metro to Monastiraki (M1 & M3) | Tip Look for Teresa Makri's little red cap among the exhibits of the Benaki Museum.

# 66 Makriyannis' Statue

*Real men wear skirts*

He stands in his kilt, sword at the ready, near the entrance to Plaka. The pedestal identifies him as General Makriyannis, 1797–1864, but he deserves a proper introduction. He was born Yannis Triantaphyllou to a poor family in Central Greece. His father died when he was 7, but by the time he was 14, he went to work for a rich man in Epirus and quickly became wealthy himself, also joining the Filiki Etairia, a secret revolutionary society. Being tall earned him the nickname, 'Long John'.

During the revolution, he fought so well, he kept being promoted until he reached the rank of full general in 1824, at just 27. Five years later, he began his memoirs, having taught himself to read and write in the meantime. They were to become not only an invaluable source of information on the war, post-war politics, people and society, but also a foundation stone of modern Greek literature. Nobel laureate George Seferis kept a copy on his desk for inspiration.

With peace, he moved to Athens, bought a farm below the Acropolis and became an outspoken politician, not afraid to criticise even King Otto. In 1852, he was arrested and condemned to death for conspiracy against the king, but released after 18 months. As so often happens, his literary merit was not hailed until long after his death and his second book, *Visions and Wonders*, was not published until 1983.

Makriyannis was such a master of words that one artist, Panagiotis Zoographos, transformed his oral descriptions of battle scenes into remarkable naif paintings. His soldiers, like his narrator, all wore kilts. Longer than those of the Evzone guards today, they were common during the Byzantine era and were chosen as the national costume by King Otto. They are said to have 400 pleats, one for every year of the Ottoman occupation. The bronze statue is the work of Yannis Pappas, a noted 20th-century sculptor.

Address Corner Vyronos and Dionysiou Areopagitou, Plaka, Athens 10558 | Getting there Metro to Acropolis (M2) and a two-minute walk | Tip Another bronze statue of a man in a kilt stands opposite the Cathedral. This is Constantinos Paleologos, the last emperor of Byzantium, 1405–1453.

# 67__Margaro

*When less is more, a Piraeus classic*

Sometimes all a restaurant needs to be a success is a speciality and two frying pans. Snuggled into an unfrequented corner of Piraeus, without even a decent view of the sea, this simple taverna meets the definition of 'no frills' but it is rarely empty. And the menu dangling from the table is superfluous because the kitchen rarely offers more than two dishes: bearded red mullet and prawns, impeccably fried, not greasy and so fresh they taste of the sea. At times, you might find fried snapper and Dublin Bay prawns, but don't count on it.

A simple village salad, topped with a slab of excellent feta, rounds out the meal no matter the season, along with fresh bread for mopping up the dressing. There's no wine list either, just the drinkable Attica white, beer and ouzo, and dessert – on the house – may be either baked halvah or syrupy orange cake. You can't even make a reservation. And yet every day, seven days a week, almost every table is occupied for lunch, dinner and in between, and has been for decades.

The hand-painted sign above the door bears the label 'oinopoleion' or wine shop, and the year 1917. But that was in a different location. Margaro from Mykonos opened this place as a taverna in 1944, right after the Nazis left, in a badly bombed, poverty-stricken Piraeus. Back then she prepared a variety of slow-cooked casseroles and baked dishes, but when her son, Lazaros, inherited the job in 1980, he slashed the menu down to the present three foods, whose quality never falters.

Today Margaro's four grandsons run the place, orchestrating the frying pans bubbling on a rudimentary two-burner stove so that you never have to wait too long for your order, no matter how crowded it is, inside and out.

Margaro has a devoted clientele of ship brokers, locals and out-of-towners. Carnivores, vegetarians and fried potato addicts had better keep their distance.

Address Hatzikyriakou 126, Piraeus 18538, +30 210 4514226 | Getting there Bus 040, 049 or 904 | Hours Daily noon–midnight, Sun until 6pm (no reservations); try to sit outside if possible and go early or at an off-hour | Tip The taverna is next to the Naval Cadet School and the sight of smartly dressed cadets, men and women, in their dazzling white uniforms, is part of its charm.

# 68 Menandrou Street
*The spicy air of multicultural Athens*

Spiralling off dingy Omonia Square you'll find yourself in a maze of streets that instantly whisk you far from Athenian ordinariness, with narrow lanes and degraded architecture, buzzing with immigrants who've manufactured a world unto itself. The air is thick with a sense of desperation for survival but also of bustling life going on as it must. Eastern Europeans may be selling counterfeit cigarettes, homeless Syrian families huddle on the pavement and Nigerian pedlars showcase imitation designer handbags. The zone can feel somewhat daunting to a westerner, particularly at night, although after various 'sweeps' by the Greek police over the years to remove the drug dealing and prostitution that had become rife in the zone, safety levels have risen.

Although Menandrou is reachable from Psyrri too, it's worth starting from Omonia Square and perambulating the surrounding streets to get a real feel for this part of town, observing examples of fascinating but sadly neglected architecture along the way.

Not at all picturesque but lively and with palpable personality, Menandrou Street is lined with traditional Pakistani barber shops where neck-cracking and vigorous head massages are part of the process, tiny hole-in-the-wall shops selling phone cards, and Chinese clothing shops. Many shop fronts are laden with chillies of every shade and degree of heat, and there's an abundance of exotic vegetables. In-the-know foodies venture here chiefly to shop in bulk at stores packed with freshly ground spices, grab a bite at fast food restaurants selling spicy kebabs or falafel, or sit at a restaurant with flavoursome, authentic, home-cooked meals that cost next to nothing. Apart from being a lively place of trade, the street reflects a microcosm of the multicultural life that has infused – and essentially restructured – the Athenian psyche over the last 20 years, changing the way more liberal locals eat, shop and celebrate diversity.

**Address** Menandrou Street, Athens 10552 | **Getting there** Metro to Omonia (M1 & M2) or Monastiraki (M1 & M3) | **Hours** Unrestricted, though best avoided at night | **Tip** Just a few streets up (not more than 10 minutes' walk) on Anaxagoras Street is Romantzo, a cultural centre, work hub and café that amalgamates the edgy grit of the area with hipster trendiness.

# 69 Mentaleaty
*Offering people a new lease on life*

Asian cuisine has become somewhat of a craze in Athens, with quality Chinese, Japanese, Indian and Thai restaurants continuously appearing on the scene. Meantaleaty, however, which opened in 2016 in the somewhat run-down area of Metaxourgeio, aims at far more than serving its customers a flavoursome Pad Thai and healthy vegan/vegetarian dishes; its greatest goal is to support individuals suffering from mental illness. Initially boosted by EU funding, it is one of several initiatives created by the social cooperative Athina-Elpis ('elpis' meaning hope) to give people with psychosocial or diagnosed psychiatric conditions rewarding employment opportunities, social benefits and an opportunity to live the kind of functional life they would normally struggle to attain.

Almost within its first few months of business, not only did the public respond very positively to the plentiful, healthy (GMO-free) menu but, crucially, the directive proved especially successful for the wellbeing of the 'patients' (who each undergo assessment before being employed). Mentaleaty was shown to help them enjoy a more balanced, positive lifestyle, living with purpose and discovering talents and a sense of community.

Easy to reach, the restaurant has a pleasantly minimalist, modern décor, an accommodating, friendly staff and a loyal clientele who return to sample the regularly upgraded menu. Athina-Elpis is made up chiefly by psychologists, psychiatrists and social care professionals who created a balanced team in Mentaleaty, made up of individuals with mental issues, volunteers and restaurant professionals. The active social enterprise has also set up (and is still running) the Luna Catering service, the Akt Café within an elderly people's unit, a professional cleaning service and a landscaping team, always with the focus on employing people with mental issues. Athina-Elpis is now planning to create more such restaurants in the near future.

Address Megalou Alexandrou 114–118, Metaxourgeio, Athens 10435, +30 213040530, www.athena-elpis.gr | Getting there Metro to Kerameikos (M3) | Hours Daily 1pm–midnight | Tip Nearby on the corner of Leonidou & Millerou Streets is the Municipal Gallery of Athens, located in a neoclassical building by architect Christian Hansen and presenting over 3,000 works by Greek artists of the 19th and 20th centuries that you can admire free of charge (Sun 10am–4pm, Tue 10am–9pm, Wed–Sat 10am–7pm).

# 70 Mentis Passementerie
*Sweatshop or life saver?*

On a nondescript street of low buildings, only the black façade of this old factory distinguishes it from its neighbours. That and a door handle made of red-and-white threads. As we stand outside, a young man stops beside us, visibly stunned. 'This is Mentis? My mother used to work for them, for years. I've got goosebumps.'

Not long ago, Athens had scores of small factories that produced textiles of all kinds. The employees 'manning' the machines were usually women, from poor urban or rural households or orphanages, like our new acquaintance's mother. And while snooty foreigners might look down on these factories as being sweatshops, these women earned both money and independence and gained a 'family' as well.

Written records maintain that Spyros Mentis founded his first factory in 1867 in Nafplio (Peloponnese) making it among the first in Greece, though his descendants put the date at 1820, even before Independence. With peace, Mentis moved to Athens to be near the Palace and a wealthy bourgeoisie who desired silk accessories no longer in fashion, such as trimmings for upholstery, braid, cords, ribbons, galloons and fringes for their salons and wardrobes. In addition to gold brocade for sword scabbards, he also designed the tassels and fringes for the Evzone guards. By the 20th century, there were several Mentis workshops in the capital.

But by the end of it, they and the others had closed. In 2011, Mentis' descendants donated their last factory to the Benaki museum, but this is no showroom of colourful threads and quaint machinery. Everything actually works, every day, and you can watch 'bobbins dancing like ballerinas' to weave a ribbon and buy a pair of tasselled earrings or a fringed sash made this year.

It is a fascinating glimpse into the vanished industrial era when people and machines worked together to create real rather than virtual things.

Address Polyfemou 6, Petralona, Athens 11854, +30 210 3478792, www.benaki.gr | Getting there Metro to Petralona (M1) and a 10-minute walk, bus 035, 049, 227, 500, 815, 838, 914, B18 or Γ18 | Hours Tue–Sat 10am–3pm | Tip Visit the Upupa Epops all-day bar a minute away at Alkmenis 7 and see how three 1930s houses around a central courtyard have been converted while keeping all the period décor. The name refers to the hoopoe, Aristophanes' king of the birds in his comedy *The Birds*.

# 71 Mid-Apollonos Street

*Where the priests and religious go shopping*

From halfway down Apollonos Street you'll start noticing a whole series of very different kinds of shops, their windows decorated with glittering religious bric-à-brac and paraphernalia. Look inside and observe jewel-encrusted crosses, hand-painted icons, churchy candelabras. Prepare yourself to see around 20 such shops ahead; on both sides of the street, you can feast your eyes on a vast array of ecclesiastical accessories and elaborately hand-crafted cloths for liturgical garments.

Reflecting the massive influence of the Greek Orthodox Church in a country where religion is a core element of national identity, the shops stream all the way to Agia Filothei Street, right behind the Metropolitan Cathedral of Athens. Some are modern and polished, while others belong to a long-gone era. The first such shop to open in 1926 belongs to renowned iconographer Konstantinos Zouvelos, whose work can be seen in churches around Greece as well as New York, San Francisco and Vancouver. With his wife and son, they create religious artefacts of all varieties; among their one-of-a-kind pieces are an elaborate, stone-encrusted silver brooch shaped like the Star of Bethlehem with an engraving of the Virgin Mary on mammoth tusk at its centre.

A little further down look out for Tasi, opened in 1986, which is jam-packed with hand-painted icons, incense burners and good luck charms featuring saints. See the many *tamata*, small metal plaques, each depicting an ailing part of the body and used as a votive offering, usually placed on a miraculous icon in a church. Also rewarding is a visit to Hiton, which centres its trade on handmade materials for every echelon of the clergy, selling everything from basic €100 plain black cotton robes to intricately designed, hand-sewn cloths in bold threads like silver or gold on velvet, satin and silk, worth up to €500 per metre.

**Address** Apollonos Street, Syntagma, Athens 10556 | **Getting there** Metro to Syntagma (M 2 & M 3) | **Hours** Regular shop hours Mon, Wed & Sat 9am – 5.30pm, Tue, Thu & Fri 9am – 7.30pm | **Tip** Light a candle in the Athens Cathedral and see the relics of the city's patron saint Agia Filothei, encased in a golden box.

# 72 Mompso

*What is a tack shop doing in the middle of Athens?*

On a street where nursery plants and heavy-duty gardening equipment crowd the pavement, and where every other shop seems related to food, Mompso stands out as indubitably the most elegant but also the most unlikely. Shepherds' crooks stand at the entrance, bags of sheep- and goatbells decorate the interior, donkey halters studded with protective evil eyes hang from the walls, but the main goods on sale here have to do with horseback riding. This is where to choose your next beautiful leather saddle, boots, gloves or jodhpurs.

Why here?

The shop's owner, Christos Triantafyllou, started his business in 2006, but the idea came to him during a trip to Morocco. There he bumped into some people who ran the factory that produces chic leather riding gear for the Paris design house Hermès. His family had already been in the leather-processing business for 100 years, so he learned all the tricks of the trade and came back with the idea of introducing a new stylish brand to Greece.

It turns out there are more riders here than you'd think, as well as people who like boots, gloves and crops for other reasons. And by being centrally located, the shop can attract customers from the countryside, where more and more people are choosing horses as a means of transport over tractors and pickups, with the price of petrol exceeding the price of oats and hay.

'Besides,' says Christos, 'I'm a man of the centre, my family's based in Psyrri, so I feel at home here. If the shop were in an exclusive suburb, I'd only get clientele from riding clubs.'

But you don't have to be a shepherd or an equestrian to enjoy this shop. People like the bells, handmade in northern Greece, for their front doors, the crooks are more fun than an ordinary cane, and what about trying your luck with a slingshot? You won't find another in Athens, since Mompso has a monopoly on the type of elastic used.

Address Athinas 33, Athens 10554, +30 210 3230670, www.mompso.com | Getting there Metro to Monastiraki (M1 & M3), and a five-minute walk | Hours Mon–Fri 9am–5pm, Sat 9am–4pm | Tip If you visit Athinas in late spring, the jacaranda trees will be in bloom, filling the sky and pavement with their exquisite mauvey-blue flowers.

# 73_ The Mount Parnitha Sanatorium

*A paranormal portal with a ghostly presence*

Athens' surrounding mountains, and especially Parnitha, the highest of all, have become vibrant hubs for sporting and leisure activities over the last few years, and you can expect to spot joggers, hikers, flower stalkers, dog lovers, rock climbers and picnic lovers in all their colour and diverse pursuits. There are even twitchers and deer spotters. What you wouldn't expect to see is a giant, forsaken old structure that could have come from the *mise-en-scène* of any horror film, a place where hundreds of tuberculosis patients died an untimely death in the early 1900s.

Once a sanatorium, the five-storey amphitheatrical structure (built in 1912) was originally the alpine branch of Athens' Evangelismos Hospital, created in the hope that the dry, highly oxygenated air could help patients. But as penicillin was sadly not brought to Greece until the mid-1950s, over 120,000 patients there died within a decade.

In 1965, the building was bought and renovated by the Greek National Tourism Organisation, and turned first into a Xenia hotel (a chain of hotels of that name were built in the country's most magnificent natural spots) and later a tourism school. Abandoned in the mid-1980s, the now vandalised building has become a popular hangout for paranormal investigators who traipse its gloomy corridors to record eerie infrared images and hair-raising sounds made by the tortured spirits eternally trapped there. Recordings can be found online.

As if the sanatorium itself is not haunting enough, right across it, on a natural expanse stands The Park of Souls. This was made in 2012 by sculptor Spyridon Dassiotis as a tribute to Greece's TB patients, featuring anthropomorphic figures carved out of charred tree trunks gathered from a devastating fire that raged on Parnitha in 2007. The faces on the randomly placed 'souls' express pain, fear, terror and sadness.

**Address** Mount Parnitha, 3km from Casino Mount Parnes, 13674 | **Getting there** By car, at 30 km north-west of Athens along the Athens-Lamia highway. If you don't want to take your car all the way to the top, you can leave it at the bottom and take the cable car. | **Hours** Unrestricted, but night-time is only for the brave! | **Tip** It's worth plotting a small hiking expedition to nearby sites like the mystical and ancient Pan's Cave or the 4th-century B.C. Phyle Fortress.

# 74 Navarinou Park

*A car park hijacked to become a community garden*

It may look like an ordinary although somewhat quirky park, a small oasis with sparkling mosaic features, cobbled pathways and a leafy tranquillity set in a cramped urban landscape. But Navarinou Park in the heart of Exarchia actually stands as a symbol for the activist, cooperative and hope-based spirit of Greeks hit by the financial crisis. The neighbourhood is often characterised as an 'anarchist' zone that breeds intellectual, non-conformist individuals and in some cases an explosively revolutionary youth culture, but is generally safe to navigate.

The park, created in 2009 by the neighbourhood's activist community (The Exarchia Residents' Initiative) along with a people's collective called 'Us, Here and Now and for All Of Us', strongly exemplifies the spirit of Exarchia's feisty residents. Once a four-storey clinic turned car park, the land's lease expired in 2008 and locals who'd had their eye on it for a few years sprang into action. They squatted on the space and eventually broke through the asphalt to turn it into what it is today. Through a democratic process, they transformed it into a gathering place for all ages; residents dedicated hands-on expertise to donate and plant trees and flowers, creating a vegetable plot, playground with a cob house and an area where film screenings, talks and performances take place in warmer months.

Quiet but never lifeless on any ordinary day, the park is a place made by the people for the people, where regular events and meetings to offer social support or organise purposeful events of all kinds continue to take place. Events like cook-outs for the homeless also take place there and active members meet every Wednesday to brainstorm ideas. Accessible during all hours, it remains the original symbol of the self-sufficiency, anti-conformity and the ability to find answers without relying on the state. While at the same time creating hope, natural beauty and creative regeneration.

Address Zoodochou Pigis 26, Exarchia, Athens 10681 | Getting there Bus 230 from Syntagma | Tip Take the few minutes' walk down to Solomou Street, and stop at White Rabbit for delicious ice cream to enjoy while reading a book picked off the packed shelves of the café's in-house library.

# 75 The Ottoman Gate

*A Muslim seminary became an infamous prison*

Opposite Vespasian's loos in the Roman Agora stands a handsome, double-arched gateway embellished with circular designs and an Arabic inscription with the name of its founder, Mehmet Fahri the Honourable. It is all that remains of a *medresse* or theological school founded in 1721 and one of the city's few relics of 376 years of Ottoman rule.

The complex must have been attractive, composed of cells arranged around a colonnaded courtyard, a large domed lecture hall and the hodja's quarters, with a kitchen and toilets to the rear. For Friday prayers, the hall served as a mosque. The cells sound like a cosy dormitory for the students, with shelves, a window and even a fireplace. On warm days, the hodja held classes under a spreading plane tree in the courtyard.

But this idyllic picture lasted less than a century. By the time Greece declared its independence in 1821, the Ottoman authorities had converted it to a prison, using the plane tree as a scaffold.

Sadly, after winning their freedom, the Greeks carried on the practice. After repairs, the new government continued incarcerating both criminals and political enemies there. Their moans so close to the busy Wheat Bazaar/market cast a pall over the district, as did the sight of bodies dangling from the tree.

But in 1843, escaped prisoners swelled the mob at the Royal Palace demanding that King Otto grant a constitution.

The prison was not closed until 1911, while the hated tree was struck by lightning in 1919, chopped down and removed, as poet Andreas Paraschos had predicted: *O plane tree of the Medresse, O sign and symbol cursed … /Bastille and dungeon of our land, the time is coming, Plane tree, /when all our people's stifled rage at last will send the woodman/to cut you down … Old age will never come to you, fire instead will burn you.* That same year the former medresse, the Bastille of Athens, was razed.

**Address** Polignotou, Monastiraki, Athens 10555 | **Getting there** Metro to Monastiraki (M 1 & M 3), and a five-minute walk | **Tip** The plane tree may no longer exist but on Diogenous Street around the corner, a historic taverna, O Platanos, commemorates it. Opened in 1933, it's shaded by mulberry trees.

# 76  Papios Bakery for the Dead

*Mourning made sweeter*

Just peering through the windows of Papios bakery one is instantly intrigued by the outlandish appearance of the 'cakes' within – most of them gleaming white and decorated with silver or gold beads, artfully crafted flowers and a cross. This is a bakery specialising in Greek Orthodox Christian memorial sweets, and is located right across from the First Cemetery of Athens. It's where the city's most prestigious families have commissioned confections honouring the memory of their dead and the most reputable place in Athens for such creations. The 'cakes' are known as *kolyva*, which Greeks have used for mourning traditions since the pre-Christian era. It looks like a cake, but instead of being sliced, its ingredients are scooped out and served in small bags. Gathering in a café after the memorial service, mourners are offered the *kolyva*, strong Greek coffee and brandy.

The base ingredient of *kolyva* is wheat, in antiquity considered a sacred metaphor for the Earth's bounty, and also symbolic as a grain that when buried, will grow again – thus signifying resurrection of the soul. The boiled wheat is mixed with other ingredients: pomegranate seeds, which lured Persephone to the underworld, are also the 'jewel' of heaven; nuts define the sprouting of the soul; raisins reflect the delight of heaven as created by the vine; blanched almonds resemble bones and the end that we all face; and finally, sugar represents the sweetness of paradise.

It's not by chance that Papios is famous for his creations. World-renowned personalities such as Queen Frederica of Greece, Eleftherios Venizelos, Aristotle Onassis, Melina Mercouri and Christodoulos, Archbishop of Greece are among the many for whom the store created its most elaborately decorated and memorable *kolyva*.

# ΠΑΠΙΟ

## 1939

### *Ποιότητα - Λεπτομέρεια*

**Address** Anapafesos 27, Mets, Athens 11636, +30 210 9220814, www.papios.gr | **Getting there** Bus 227 from Syntagma or Monastiraki; trolley 4 | **Hours** Sat, Mon & Wed 9am–5pm, Tue, Thu & Fri 9am–3pm & 5–8.30pm | **Tip** Go from death to life at artsy Café Odeon on Markou Mousourou a few streets away. In the evening, you might catch some live music.

# 77 The Parrot Colony

*Tropical birds find a home in the National Gardens*

Don't be surprised if you hear the odd chattering or shriek or squawk among the twitters and chirps as you stroll through the National Gardens, originally designed by Queen Amalia as the royal gardens. You're not imagining it, nor is it a distortion of the car horns from the traffic outside: that *was* indeed a parrot that you heard.

It's a well-known secret that this 15-hectare wooded park in the midst of the Greek capital is home to a sizeable colony of wild parrots, from a fluctuating number of parakeets to the odd cockatoo. They're not always easily visible: even larger species like the ring-necked parakeet (*Psittacula krameri*) and Amazon parrots with their mostly green plumage are hard to spot amidst the foliage. But if you let your ears guide your eyes, you'll be able to pick them out on the higher branches, especially in the area around the Botanical Museum where there are a number of trees from Asia – a region native to parrots. And while they also populate other parks around Athens, this community is one of the most stable and easy to spot.

Birdwatchers have always delighted in the National Gardens. Its size and the variety of flora in what was originally a palace park designed in the mid-1800s by Queen Amalia is home to a range of species, from the wryneck woodpecker (*Jynx torquilla*) to *Troglodytes troglodytes*, one of the smallest birds in Europe and the only wren species on the continent. But parrots? Ornithologists believe the colonies were formed by caged parrots that escaped or, in some cases, were released by owners once their pet's novelty wore off. This theory is supported by the existence of one or two smaller colonies in small, suburban wooded parks, but the one in the National Gardens is the largest. Though tropical, the parrots seem to have adapted to the cold winter temperatures and a rather different diet – although their tastes seem to draw them to the leaves and berries of plants endemic to their original habitats.

Address Amalias 1, Athens 11634, +30 210 7215019 (entrances also on Vas. Sofias, Irodou Attikou and in Zappeion Park) | Getting there Metro to Syntagma (M2 & M3); tram; bus 2, 3, 4, 11, 12, 40, 54, 165, 203, 204, 209, 224 or 732 | Hours Daily 6am–5.30pm (varies with season, closing time around sunset) | Tip Traces of a 400-square-metre mosaic unearthed on the Vas. Sofias side have been identified as the atrium of a Roman villa.

# 78 A Patriarch's Tomb
*Skullduggery after a martyr's death*

On Easter Day, 1821, a month after Greece declared its independence from the Ottomans, the Patriarch, Gregory V, was assassinated in Constantinople. Although he had condemned the declaration, fearing reprisals against his congregation, the Turks arrested him after the mass, hanged him and left him, in his gold vestments, outside the Patriarchate for two days. Then his corpse was dragged through the streets and dumped into the Bosphoros. A Greek sailor recognised the body, salvaged it and sailed off to Odessa, where it was interred.

Fifty years later, the Russian government offered the Patriarch's bones to the King of Greece for reburial in his native land. But to avoid offending the Sultan, they would have to be transported overland, avoiding Ottoman territory, which included the Balkans.

The Greek ambassador, Alexandros Rangavis, managed to convince the Grand Vizir that the remains should be shipped direct to Athens through the Bosphoros. Initially, the official believed they belonged in Constantinople, but Rangavis pointed out that such a shrine would attract unwelcome hordes of Orthodox pilgrims, while were they to be installed in Athens, their arrival would be hailed with vast enthusiasm, hymns and insults to the Turks, but the excitement would soon stop and all would be forgotten.

Rangavis arranged an elaborate cover up so the ship would not be detected, only to have his orders ignored, but clever diplomacy kept the peace.

Eventually a new sarcophagus for Gregory V was laid in the Athens Cathedral to great fanfare but Rangavis was right. Few people even know of its existence. White marble with gold ornamentation, it depicts the bier in a boat manned by two angels against a sky-blue background, the two-headed eagle of Byzantium and the Patriarch's mitre.

Gregory V was made a saint and the Patriarchate's front gate has been locked since Easter 1821.

Address Athens Cathedral, Mitropoleos, Athens 10556, +30 210 3221308 | Getting there Metro to Syntagma (M2 & M3) or Monastiraki (M1 & M3), and a five- to seven-minute walk | Hours Daily 6.30am–7pm | Tip The Little Cathedral, a 12th-century church built on the site of an ancient temple and incorporating plaques and artefacts from early Christian churches, has much more appeal than the vast 19th-century Cathedral next to it.

# 79 Piraeus Archaeological Museum

*A museum that doesn't want to be visited*

Compared with its stately counterpart in Athens, this museum could be a school or a drab government office building. There's no hint of the beautifully displayed treasures inside, while the scant remains of an ancient theatre next door preside over a jumble of marble spare parts crowded against the fence. The interior is a different story.

A replica of the Lion of Piraeus, the statue which gave the port its mediaeval name Porto Leone, stands near the entrance. The Venetians stole the original. Below it looms the Kallithea funeral monument, worth studying before you rush upstairs to see this small museum's main attractions, four extraordinary bronze statues.

The monument was commissioned by Nikeratos, a 'foreigner' from Asia Minor in the early 4th century B.C. It inspired the same reaction as *nouveaux riches* villas and gold Cadillacs do today.

The bronzes instead are a paean to our higher side. Only 35 such life- or larger-than-life-sized pieces from the ancient world are known to exist. And these remained unseen for two millennia until 1959 when workmen repairing the Piraeus sewerage network lifted them from the muck, where they had been hidden during the Roman general Sulla's notorious plundering rampage in 87 B.C. The oldest and rarest is a 6th-century rendering of Apollo as a youth or *kouros*. Most other archaic figures are marble. Beyond him stand three goddesses, 4th-century masterpieces. Two represent Artemis, one delicate and eroded, one with an elaborate inlaid quiver; the third is an imposing Athena, with crested helmet. Take a close look at their hairdos, elaborate robes and white eyeballs.

Completing the collection is a large mask depicting tragedy, with gaping eyes and mouth, wild snakelike curls for hair, tighter whorls for his beard.

**Address** Harilaou Trikoupi 31, Piraeus 18536, +30 210 4521598 | **Getting there** Metro to Piraeus (M 1), and 20-minute walk; bus 049, 300, 904, 906 or 909 | **Hours** Tue – Sun 8am – 3pm | **Tip** Walk down to Zea and see the vast array of sailing and motor yachts docked there, another incredible display of wealth. It used to be known as Passalimani, the Pasha's harbour, but was changed to Zea in the '70s to be more politically correct.

# 80 Piraeus Municipal Theatre
*Gleaming contrast to the scruffy port*

When the Municipal Theatre opened in 1895, it was grander than any theatre in Athens. It had been in the works since 1882, when the funds initially allotted for its construction, 200,000 drachmas, amounted to almost two-thirds of the city's budget. But the ambitious project was envisaged as the symbol of Piraeus, so money was no object. Naturally, like all high-minded ventures, it ended not only overbudget but costing more than the city coffers held – 900,000 drachmas – requiring a loan from the National Bank.

But everyone agreed that it was a jewel and the inauguration attracted foreign as well as Greek dignitaries, not to mention ordinary residents of the port town.

The architect, Ioannis Lazarimos, from Piraeus himself, but a graduate of the Berlin Polytechnic and the École des Beaux-Arts in Paris, modelled the interior on that city's Odéon-Théâtre de l'Europe. The façade, neoclassical with Corinthian columns, looks more Roman than Greek, but the stage is one of the few examples of the baroque style that is still functioning.

During its heyday, almost every big name in Greek theatre directed or performed there, but during emergencies it played other roles. The French army requisitioned it during World War I, while with the population exchange of 1922, it housed refugees from Asia Minor, who created little apartments in the boxes. Sometimes it also gave space to labour syndicates, the Commerce Club and a guard headquarters. It recovered from Allied bombing in 1944 and again from the earthquake of '81, but the more severe earthquake of '99 damaged it further.

Now, meticulously restored, it reopened in 2015 in the presence of the Greek president, prime minister and local mayor. The magnificent golden stage, boxes, balconies, painted and moulded ceilings and the huge chandelier alone are worth the price of admission.

Address Iroon Polytechniou 32, Piraeus 18535, +30 210 4143310, www.dithepi.gr |
Getting there Metro to Piraeus (M1), and bus 040 to Korai Square or 10–15-minute
walk, bus X80 from Syntagma, bus B1, 049 or 904 | Hours Open only for performances,
but try to peep inside during a matinée | Tip The big square structure opposite the
theatre has worn its camouflage shroud for several decades. A never-completed project of
a former mayor, it was to have been a school, the Town Hall, and a courthouse. Don't
hold your breath for its completion.

# 81 Plastikourgeio

*A symbol of the city's growing eco-awareness*

On the border between edgy Exarchia and genteel Kolonaki you'll find a place that offers intelligent, creative and sustainable solutions for a plastic-free existence. In the front of the store there is everything from reusable water bottles and coffee cups, stainless steel straws, eco-friendly shopping bags, zero waste travelling kits, trendy cloth lunch bags, bamboo toothbrushes and biodegradable plastic-free sponges. There's also a selection of charming home décor items and innovative jewellery made by collaborating local designers out of plumbing, electrical and computer materials.

At the back of the shop is the lab, modelled on an upcycling project called Precious Plastic created by Dutch designer Dave Hakkens; his idea has already enabled individuals globally to set up their own labs with homemade machines. Ask the owners Daphne Marneli (a Greek archaeologist with a museum background) and Fran Vardas (an Andalusian marine biologist and environmental conservator) to show you the exciting equipment they've made and use daily. Things like the shredder, and the extrusion, injection and compression machines as well as a 3D printer are used to create new functional and decorative items from plastic brought in by neighbours and clients, who want to be part of the eco-activism the shop is promoting.

Vardas and Marneli were inspired to create Plastikourgeio after a holiday on an island where the tap water was unsuitable for drinking. As there were no recycling bins around, they collected all the water bottles they used and were alarmed by the sheer quantity of plastic they'd gathered in the back of their car. Apart from opening the store/lab in 2017, they've already run a series of educational, practical community workshops and are reaching out to Athens' cafés and restaurants to participate in cutting down on plastic use via their Plastic-Free Drinks Campaign.

Address Asklipiou 51, Exarchia, Athens 10680, +30 210 0443356, www.plastikourgeio.com | Getting there Metro to Panepistimio (M2) or Agiou Nikolaou bus stop via buses 025, 026 or 027 | Hours Mon & Wed 10.30am–5pm, Tue 10.30am–7pm, Thu & Fri 10.30am–8pm | Tip Further along Asklipiou Street (number 3) is the Kostis Palamas Museum, dedicated to the renowned Greek poet from the 1800s who wrote the words for the Olympic Hymn.

# 82 Plateia Avissinias/ Yousouroum

*The Athens Flea Market by its other names*

Eventually, most visitors to Athens pass through this square in the heart of Monastiraki. During the week, its shops display their wares on the pavement, from hefty pieces of furniture to delicate bric-à-brac, medals, musical instruments, silver spoons – just about anything you can imagine. On Sundays, vendors, collectors and gypsies bring more offerings, treasures or junk, second-hand clothes, antiquated radios, books, records and trivia of all sorts. It's almost impassable and the jumble sale spills into the side streets up to the Thissio metro station.

But the tradition and the names of this square have their own story. It was first called Auction Square in 1910, after a site a few streets away where second-hand goods were auctioned on Sunday mornings.

The connection to Abyssinia is vague. Some sources link it to the presence of a small colony of Ethiopians who lived nearby. Others say it was in honour of Emperor Haile Selassie who visited Athens in 1924 and offered aid to refugees from Asia Minor. In any case, it did not officially acquire the name Avissinias until the 1980s.

Meanwhile, Greeks had been calling the used-goods bazaar Yousouroum since the mid-1800s. In fact, the word has entered the vocabulary as 'second-hand shop'. But it's really the family name of a Sephardic Jewish immigrant, Bohor Yousouroum, who set up a clothing store nearby in 1863. His ancestors had fled Spain during the Inquisition for the Ottoman Empire. When Greece won its independence, Bohor emigrated to Athens. But on Sundays, he moved his wares to the main bazaar. In time, people started saying, 'Where shall we go? To Yousouroum to shop'.

When he died, his sons expanded the business, which became the core of the Jewish community in Athens, and gave its name to the square.

Address Plateia Avissinias, Ifestou 2, Monastiraki, Athens 10555 | Getting there Metro to Monastiraki (M 1 & M 3), and a three-minute walk | Tip Athens' first synagogue was located in the home of the Yousouroum family at Karaiskaki 1 and Ermou. Today there are two functioning synagogues opposite each other a few streets west at Melidoni 5 and 8. The older one (8, 1905) opens only on high holy days.

# 83 Portrait of Loukanikos

*The Riot Dog lives for ever in the heart of Athens*

As an expressive, somewhat anarchic people with a soul-tapestry woven of democratic ideals, Greeks love to protest. When the Eurozone crisis reared its ugly head in 2009, Greece began to hit the global headlines. In the ensuing years, Athens became a battlezone, with hooded, bare-chested anarchists in violent face-offs against shielded, helmeted riot police. Shop windows were smashed, Molotov cocktails launched, and Athenians shut their windows to keep the tear gas out of their homes. Meanwhile, Loukanikos ('sausage') the dog, one of Athens' multitude of strays, was always on the front lines at these dramatic events; siding with protestors, he barked aggressively at the cops, unhindered by rocks, kicks or flames.

Worldwide, the media picked up on this canine anarchist. In 2011, *TIME* magazine featured Loukanikos on its front cover. The song 'The Riot Dog' by David Rovics was written in his honour and the four-legged warrior even inspired the documentary *Dogs of Democracy* by Mary Zournazi, in which he's described as the 'Che Guevara of Greece' and 'an ally of the Greek people of all ideologies'. In 2012 he retired from his energetic street life and was adopted by a family who offered him the loving care he deserved. He died peacefully in his sleep in 2014.

Apart from its reputation for protests, modern Athens is also known for its graffiti, a liberal practice that dates back millennia in Greece. After Loukanikos' death, street artists who knew the brave hound well dedicated a giant wall portrait in his memory, titled *All Dogs Go to Heaven*. Billy Gee, Alex Martinez and N_Grams say they wanted to bring a smile to the faces of passers-by.

Despite his world fame, few know that they can visit him here. And indeed, the wonderfully expressive and instagrammable portrait inspires many emotions in any observer – from the superficial to the profoundly idealistic.

Address Riga Pallamidou 4 & Sarri Street, Psyrri, Athens 10554 | Getting there Metro to Monastiraki (M 1 & M 3) | Tip Head a few streets up to Evripidou Street for a bite to eat in the courtyard of Greek deli / restaurant Ta Karamanlidika Tou Fani, with an incredible, authentic meze menu.

# 84 Prosfygika Complex
*Cultural history in dire degradation*

Alexandras Avenue is noisy and unattractive, but it's definitely not lacking in character. There is the Panathinaikos (PAO) football stadium, covered in photos of national football heroes, graffiti of skeletons and the PAO symbol, the four-leaf clover. Across the avenue is the large white building of the capital's police head-quarters, and further on the imposing Supreme and Civil Criminal Courthouse.

Across from the sprawling PAO stadium is a row of derelict, low-rise apartment blocks that look like they're made of crumpled brown paper. You'd think that the row of Bauhaus-inspired buildings was abandoned, if it wasn't for signs of life on tiny balconies – a red beach umbrella and a row of laundry flapping in the wind. This is the Prosfygika housing complex, built by the state in 1934 to house Greek refugees who fled to the mother country after the Asia Minor Catastrophe of 1922. Exploring further you'll be amazed by its sheer size – the whole complex consists of 6 rows of buildings and 228 flats. A progressive project when first erected, the flats were designed to be modest but functional, with large communal spaces

The buildings have come under threat of demolition several times throughout the decades; in 1967 the junta planned to knock them down to create a park, and in 2000 the state considered destroying the complex to create an attractive green space in lieu of the upcoming Olympic Games. By 2005, the Hellenic Real Estate Corporation had bought out 180 of the flats but vehement protests in defence of their historical value succeeded in having them listed in 2008. Although some of the original inhabitants still doggedly live here, many of the vacated flats have been filled by homeless squatters, artists, rights activists, drug addicts and recent refugees. Controversy continues to bubble over what the fate of Prosfygika will be.

Address Alexandras Avenue 165–169, Athens 11472 | Getting there Metro to Ambelokipi (M3); bus A7 | Tip Go up Panormou Street (number 3) just off Alexandras to popular Peinirli Ionias to try Greece's calzone-style snack with a choice of fillings.

# 85 Pyrgos Vasilissis

*A modern farm fit for a queen*

Independent, adventurous and nature-loving, Queen Amalia liked to explore Athens on horseback, and when during one of her promenades she came upon a fertile valley of the Kifissos river, she was enchanted by it. She bought it in 1838 from two Englishmen who had already planted fruit trees and a vineyard, with the vision of creating a model agricultural unit with modern farming methods.

The Queen's Tower or Pyrgos Vasilissis, as it is known today, is located in the unremarkable neighbourhood of Ilion. Visitors to this lush spot are always awestruck by the enchanting change of scene from urban Athens. The 30-hectare land includes manicured gardens, Romantic-style fountains, statues, flowers of all varieties, a vineyard producing top quality organic wine, stables and farmed land including olive groves and fruit trees. Although such beauty is a feast for the eyes in itself, the jewel in the crown is Queen Amalia and King Otto's summer villa; the Gothic-style, fairy-tale castle was inspired by the Hohenschwangau Castle in Otto's native Bavaria and designed by French architect Francois-Louis-Florimond Boulanger. It has ramparts, arched windows and doorways and polygonal towers. Its interiors are exquisitely decorated, with magnificent ceiling art in every room as well as elegant furnishings, also designed by Boulanger. Shoes come off in the reception hall to preserve the stunning handmade parquet floor in a particularly impressive recently renovated room; beautiful ceiling art and vibrant blue silk walls are embellished with resplendent gold details.

Amalia's act of setting up the farm created an ecological legacy that continues to this day. The owners of the estate welcome visitors for a tour of the tower and grounds and organise wine tastings, while the Organisation Earth NGO has also been set up there, running educational workshops via their Earth Centre.

Address Dimokratias Avenue 67, Ilion 13122, +30 210 2313607, www.pyrgosvasilissis.gr |
Getting there Suburban railway to Pyrgos Vasilissis and then bus to Menidi; bus A 10,
B 10 or 735 | Hours By appointment only; to book, call +30 210 2313697 | Tip Buy a bottle
of wine from the vineyard and have a picnic with you to eat at the Antonis Tritsis Ecology
Park next door.

# 86 The Queen's Houses

*Royal facelift turns shanty town to alpine village*

Petralona doesn't get much tourist traffic beyond the spillover from Thissio's bars, but a stroll along the Philopappou ring road offers a curious sight: a cluster of wood-trimmed two-storey stone cottages with iron railings and brick chimneys that are the hallmark of alpine architecture.

A city's history is told by its architecture. Built in the 1950s, the 160-odd cottages are perhaps the earliest effort at gentrification, not by residents but by the Royal Charity controlled by Queen Frederica, granddaughter of Wilhelm II and probably most controversial of all the Greek monarchs. The settlement was built as housing for some 800-plus refugee families living in a shanty town huddled inside the disused Philopappos quarry – a sight that reportedly disturbed Frederica and was not in keeping with the image of post-war Greece that the government sought to project. Much of the stone was demolition waste from the former Naval Academy nearby, with timber cut from trees on the adjacent hillside. Each house was allocated an area of 55 square metres, two storeys and an enclosed courtyard. Additional housing for refugees was provided a decade later, in 1967, by the Public Works Ministry's Public Housing Service. It, too, is an unusual and quite remarkable example of 1960s architecture. Designed by Elli Vasilikioti as a complex for low-income families, its 60-odd apartments are arrayed along four storeys and linked by open-air corridors along the front. Walk to the corner to note its most unusual feature: the building traces the hill's curve.

Many Greeks believe the name Petralona is from the stone (petra) quarry but it derives from the stone threshing floors (alonia) that were once used to thresh grain located there. But old-timers claim that it's from the stone-throwing fights pitched by local youths against urchins (alani) from neighbouring districts.

**Address** Area between the 77th Elementary School (Odos Troon), Iperionos, Navarhou Voulgari and Stisikleous, Athens 11852 | **Getting there** Metro to Thissio (M 1), then a five-minute walk | **Tip** The now-hip Petralona district was the setting of Alekos Alexandrakis' 1961 film *Synikia to Oneiro* (Dream Neighbourhood), which was heavily censored for showing the city's squalor.

# 87 __ Remember Fashion
*Original cult designs loved by A-list rockers*

Remember is a cult fashion store that you can't easily forget. Its entry stairway sets the tone as it's splattered with graffiti slogans like 'public apathy' and 'we are ruled by none'. It was opened in Plaka in post-junta Athens (1978) by eccentric artist Dimitris Tsouanatos, whose original designs immediately appealed to Greek youths fuelled by the desire to break out of a sombre traditional mould and express themselves through their style of clothes. At the time, the punk movement was also starting to yell itself into being, making the store even more alluring to Greek customers seeking to connect with a more Western sense of assertiveness.

The 1980s fashion continues to be a running theme in the designs even today, but Tsouanatos' overall love of creative youth culture and music has heavily coloured his work – tones of New Wave, Rock, Metal, Rave and Electronica music genres are visible. Almost everything in the shop, from T-shirts with painted faces or original photos to Elvis-style gold lamé jumpsuits or studded-leather-strap S&M gear, as well as accessories like hats, shoes and jewellery are his original designs.

Tsouanatos, who is also an accomplished sculptor and painter and has published three poetry books with his own collage artwork, has become a cult figure among artists in Greece and around the world. Most pieces are one-of-a-kind or made (in recent years also by his son) in small quantities, and this too pleases individuals who enjoy a unique style. It's fascinating but not by chance that the shop is regularly visited not only by local artists and fashionistas but even Hollywood A-listers like style icon Chloë Sevigny, the cast of *Orange Is the New Black*, Lana Del Rey and a multitude of rockers like the Ramones, Scorpions and Debbie Harry. Photos of all customers, famous or not, are saved in stacks of photo albums you can leaf through.

Address Eschilou 28, Psyrri, Athens 10554, +30 210 3216409 | Getting there Metro to Monastiraki (M1 & M3) | Hours Mon–Sat 10am–9pm | Tip Continue your experience of idiosyncratic Athens by having breakfast in bed at Spiti Mas, a café-bistro on Navarchou Apostoli Street (five minutes' walk) modelled on home living.

# 88 Rizopoulos Coffee Roasters

*Waking up to the perfect brew*

Just a sniff of freshly brewed coffee will jolt you awake, but a whiff of Greek coffee is more like a velvet caress to the olfactory senses – rich, smooth and soothing. And although it's been edged out of fashion by frappé and cappuccino, Greek coffee is still the only coffee many older Greeks will drink.

For a taste of this time-honoured Greek tradition, head down to Rizopoulos, a family-run business that has been buying, roasting, selling and brewing coffee for over a century in the same premises near City Hall. Sacks of coffee beans crowd the floor, waiting to be roasted and then scooped into the grinder to be turned into the fragrant powder stirred into the *briki*.

Although the shop has expanded and diversified into other products since 1901, its core business is still Greek coffee and no matter how busy, staff always willingly take time to explain the dos and don'ts of brewing it properly. *Sketos* (plain), *glykys vrastos* (sweet and boiled), *me kaimaki* (with foam): for every technique, the key is patience. Greek coffee should not be rushed. The water should be heated slowly – ideally over a hearth – and the coffee added at the start so the powdery grounds have time to develop and release their flavour. Stir only once, when you add the coffee to the water. And think small, from the brewing pot to the serving cup to preserve the aroma and taste.

Patience is also the secret to enjoying Greek coffee. It's sipped, savoured at breakfast and late afternoon, not guzzled throughout the day. Staff will also dissuade you from buying more than 200 grams, with 100 to 150 grams being the average quantity sold to customers. Maybe it's not the most efficient business model, but for Rizopoulos, the cheery 'see you next week!' called out to customers has served it well.

Address Stefanou Streit 1, Athens 11634, +30 210 3218428 | Getting there Metro to Omonia (M1 & M2); bus 35, 227 or 500 | Hours Mon–Thu 7am–4pm, Fri 7am–5pm, Sat 7am–3pm | Tip Greek coffee is served with a loukoumi on the side. See how they're made at Loukoumia Vomvilla (Theodoritou Vrestheni 7, Neos Kosmos).

# 89__ The Rock Slide

*Smoothing the way to parenthood*

Visitors, understandably, are drawn to the Hill of the Acropolis but in antiquity the three other hills of the limestone formation on which Athens sat were of equal, if not greater, importance. The most underappreciated today is the Hill of the Nymphs, known as the site of the National Observatory, which was built in 1842. But it is also the one that was consistently used, from antiquity, when it hosted shrines to Pan and Apollo, to modern times when its caves provided both water and an escape route for defenders barricaded on the Acropolis. And in mediaeval times, the hill was believed to be the home not of nymphs but the sisters Plague, Cholera and Smallpox – which may explain why the Greeks tossed the corpses of those sentenced to death off its ledge.

But across millennia, the hill's value to the city has not been the panoramic view it offers, but its stone. The hill's marble continued to be quarried – illegally – through the 19th century and the rocks are riddled with the marks of this activity. Except one: the 'sliding rock'. You can spot the smooth boulder a few metres from the site of the 11th-century church of Agia Marina (now, mostly underground and only occasionally accessible through the larger church). Pregnant women 'slid' down the rock whose smooth surface was said to ensure a smooth birth. It's a custom rooted in both mythology and orthodoxy as Saint Marina is the protector of children. Childless women also rubbed against the rock so they would conceive smoothly.

The best, albeit not the quickest, way to reach Agia Marina and the rock is to follow the formal path from the Dionysiou Areopagitou past Agios Dimitrios Loubardiaris, then veer towards the observatory. On the right is a 500-metre footpath that winds among pines. It is the Koile road – a recently excavated section of an ancient road linking Athens to Piraeus. Look for the water channel and grave markers inscribed with the names of the deceased from an adjacent cemetery.

Address Lofos Nymfon, Athens 11851 | **Getting there** Metro to Thissio (M1) | **Hours** Daily 8am–3pm (except specified holidays) | **Tip** This hill has been used for observing the skies since antiquity when the astronomer Meton set up his heliotropion. Look for its traces near the scarp where Zeus was worshipped.

# 90 Salt Cave of Glyfada

*Halotherapy in the city*

Just 45 minutes' drive southwards from central Athens one can find endless coastlines, some of them swimmable, to bask in the sunshine and take in cleansing ozonic breezes. However, for a deeply intensive and therapeutic experience you can visit the Salt Cave of Glyfada where less than an hour of just sitting in there equates to three days at the seaside. Heading to the Salt Cave, the only one of its kind in Greece, you may be a bit put off by the desolate quiet of the City Plaza shopping centre, today half-vacated because of the financial crisis. But upon entering the 'cave' itself, the trek over immediately feels worthwhile.

Lit up mesmerically in shades of soft orange, the Salt Cave, made up entirely of tons of salt mined in Poland (with a blend of Dead Sea salt) is designed to offer a multitude of benefits via halotherapy ('halo' comes from the Greek for 'salt'): detoxification of the respiratory system, rebalancing of the nervous system and a boost to the immune system are just a few of them. With a rich mineral content and potent antimicrobial and antibacterial properties, concentrated salt can help soothe skin ailments such as psoriasis and eczema, regulate sleep patterns and even ease chronic conditions such as asthma and rheumatism.

Many come here simply to sit in the zero gravity chairs that prop up the legs while listening to the sound of water trickling down the two salt fountains that are installed especially to retain humidity, in a temperature of 22°C. Others throw in a relaxing Thai or oil massage by expert therapists or beauty treatment to the experience, or participate in a weekly yoga class to stretch and breathe in the healing air. The Salt Cave also organises monthly events like sound baths, in which Tibetan singing bowls and gongs create otherworldly harmonies that fit perfectly with the womb-like vibe of the cave itself.

**Address** Vouliagmenis Avenue 85 and Antheon, in the City Plaza Mall, Athens 16674, +30 210 9642550, www.glyfadasaltcave.com.gr | **Getting there** Metro to Elliniko (M2) and then bus 171, A3 or X97 to Antheon | **Hours** Mon, Wed & Fri 9.30am–8pm, Tue & Thu 9.30am–9.15pm, Sat 9.30am–5pm | **Tip** Stay on the health-track by walking (seven minutes) to Yi, Athens' only raw food, zen-décor, top-quality restaurant.

# 91__The Servant of Philo

*Wine and robotics in Ancient Greece*

The world may well know that the Greeks inspired philosophy, democracy, political thought and medicine, but little to nothing is known of their incredible and progressive feats in the area of technology. In an age when humanity is anticipating, debating, even dreading the inevitable takeover of life by robots, The Servant of Philo is an unmissable thing to see in Athens. The generally unknown, world's first robot was a life-sized maiden who served wine – with the perfect mixture of water as the ancient Greeks deemed drinking wine straight as dangerous and somewhat barbaric – to symposium guests. She was the brainchild of Philo of Byzantium, who lived in the 3rd century B.C., and who invented the water mill. In the cavity of her chest are two containers, one of water and one of wine that connect via tubes and are poured through a pitcher she holds in her right hand, once a guest had placed his cup into her left hand.

The Kotsanas Museum of Ancient Greek Technology where the blank-eyed servant stands, presents around 145 exhibits made by mechanical engineer Kostas Kotsanas, who dedicated over 20 years to studying Greek, Latin and Arabic texts and paintings on ancient vessels. He has recreated over 300 millennia-old inventions, most by hand and every one of them awe-inspiring. They include the first alarm system by Heron, as well as his revolutionary aeolosphere (the precursor of the steam engine), Plato's alarm clock, flying machines, automatic theatres and technology for telecommunications, war, astronomy, mathematics, building, agriculture and the arts.

The surprises never end: walking upstairs to an exhibition of musical instruments and a café with classical board games, you'll be making music. Each step plays a note from the 'Song of Seikilos' (written by a widower for his late wife), the world's oldest surviving musical composition.

Address Pindarou 6, Kolonaki, Athens 10671, +30 211 4110044, www.kotsanas.com | Getting there 10 minutes' walk from Syntagma Square; bus 060, 203, 204, 224 or Λ5 to nearby Kanari Street | Hours Daily 9am–5pm | Tip After seeing the first cinema ever invented, head to the Aglaia Mitropoulou, a little further down (Kanari 1) to learn about the evolution of Greek filmmaking.

# 92 Skateboarders' Piste

*Athens youth ramp up the grinds to classical 'airs'*

The skateboarder whizzing the wrong way down Archelaou Street with its hip cafes can only be headed to one place: the Athens Conservatory. It's not a student late for class, but a rider heading to a practice meet at the conservatory's piazza-like lobby.

The metallic trundle of wheels punctuated by the cymbal-like clash of wood against surface marking a turn is music to a rider's ear, although not necessarily to the ears of the students practising their scales and their Skalkottas.

For nearly four decades, the Athens Conservatory was a ghost building – stigmatised as a creation of the military junta that seized power in 1967 and collapsed in 1974, even though the Conservatory itself was founded in 1871 and the building had been commissioned in 1959. Delays pushed construction back a decade, but the building was never completed, just its shell. Ioannis Despotopoulos' marvellously minimalist design – which houses 35 classrooms, 2 audiotoria, a library and concert hall – fell into near-ruin. It stood abandoned from 1976 until the early 2010s, that is when it was discovered by the city's skateboarders and break-dancers as a meeting place.

The ground-level arcade was the perfect space: a 130-metre smooth marble track, set back from the street yet easily accessible, and protected from the rain. After school and on holidays, riders met here in unofficial competitions and showcases. And it was as if their presence breathed life back into the edifice, which, thanks to the Conservatory's new director, underwent a complete renovation and was finally 'inaugurated' in 2016.

Skateboarders and musical scholars now coexist as the Conservatory evolves into a school for the performing arts. It is a wonderful facility, with stunning concert and exhibition areas, and perhaps the most underrated cultural venue in the Greek capital. By everyone except the riders, that is.

**Address** Rigillis and Vas. Georgiou B 17–19, Athens 10675, +30 210 7240673 | **Getting there** Metro to Evangelismos (M3); bus 10 or 550 | **Tip** The Hellenic Children's Museum ('please touch our exhibits') also has space in the complex.

# 93  Soutsos-Rallis House

*The mansion in plain sight that no one ever sees*

In any other neighbourhood, this two-storey neoclassical mansion with its elegant staircase would attract attention, but here it has to compete with the 'Trilogy' across the way: the Academy, the University and the National Library, monuments erected in the mid-1800s to reflect the glorious heritage of the new nation's capital. It is also overshadowed, literally, by a modern glass office block.

For it to be there at all, it must have a story.

And it starts with the first owner's family, in Epirus early in the Ottoman era, when a man named Drakos made his way to Constantinople and inserted himself into the Sublime Porte. His descendants changed their name to Soutsos and acquired wealth and position in the empire, as did so many capable Greeks. One became ruler of Moldavia-Wallachia, and his son, Bucharest-born Skarlatos, attended military academy in Munich with a scholarship awarded by King Ludwig. Later, Greece's first president, Capodistrias, appointed him professor at the new military academy in Athens and he became *aide-de-camp* to King Otto and Minister of the Army, presiding over the liberation of Thessaly from the Turks in 1881.

Meanwhile, the new capital was becoming grander. Panepistimiou, the city's widest street, was now a boulevard lined with grand mansions, although the Archbishop ruled it too remote for its new cathedral.

Skarlatos married into an old Byzantine family, built the house and raised two children there. His son, Dimitrios, went on to become mayor of Athens at 33, serving for two consecutive terms (1879–1887). Responsible for major public works (the reservoir, the market), he was scorned by the elite who called him the 'mayor of the shoeshine boys' because of his fondness for the poor. When he died in 1904, his widow sold the house to another political family, the Rallis, who gave Greece two prime ministers.

Address Corner of Panepistimiou and Korai, Athens 10564 | Getting there Metro to Panepistimio (M2) | Hours Viewable from the outside only | Tip Laying this street was no piece of cake since it was full of boulders and Korai turned into a river during heavy rains. Its official name, written on signposts, is El. Venizelou but no one calls it that.

# 94__St John on the Column
*A stake from an older worship*

Most churches in Greece, especially the early ones, were built with materials from dismantled pre-Christian temples or over these ancient places of worship. But Ai Yiannis, a small church sandwiched between Evripidou Street's market buildings, looks like it was dropped on one. How else to explain the marble column with the Corinthian capital poking out of the slanted brick roof?

The church, among the city's earliest, dates from the 5th or 6th century. True to practice, it sits on a temple dedicated to the ancient god of healing, Asclepius. In keeping with these roots, the church is dedicated to St John the Baptist, also a healer. Logic suggests that when the church was built, the column was so firmly embedded that it was impossible to remove. But local lore offers another account. Towards the end of his life, St John is said to have insisted on installing the column to tether diseases. The faithful would then tie three knots in a ribbon, attach it to the column, and repeat a prayer-chant three times asking St John to 'release' them from their illness. The story doesn't really stand up to either simple mathematics or Christian dogma as it's suspiciously pagan, but it is charming.

Even with the column, the small single-nave basilica is easy to miss. It's set slightly back from the street, in a small courtyard whose shady trees often hide most of the building, sometimes even the gate. Indeed, its clapboard exterior and aluminium shingle extensions conjure village dwelling more than church – except on holy days, when it's decked with flags and Orthodox insignia. The wood templon inside also has a rural feel. Neither ornate nor especially pretty, it is crammed with icons of a bevy of saints. But it's not the icons on which worshippers place votives: it's the column. To this day, the faithful tie ribbons around its base seeking a cure from St John.

**Address** Evripidou 70, Psyrri, Athens 10554 | **Getting there** Metro to Monastiraki (M1 & M3); bus 35, 227 or 500 | **Hours** Sun mornings, Mon–Fri mornings and Orthodox holy days | **Tip** Pop in at Trakas Candlemakers (Aristofanous 28) for a glimpse of how church candles are shaped from huge vats of melting beeswax to rows of tapers hung by their wicks to dry.

# 95___ Stani

*Yoghurt like ewe have never tasted*

Fifty years ago, milk bars in the Athens–Piraeus megalopolis vastly outnumbered bars that served alcohol. In those days, there were as many as 1,600 such places, where customers of all ages would pop in for a bowl of yoghurt, rice pudding or *krema* (milk pudding) accompanied by a tumbler of cold water or a thimble of Greek coffee. If this habit sounds peculiar, you haven't tasted real Greek yoghurt. Don't be fooled; it has nothing to do with the mass-produced versions found in supermarkets.

Mostly made from ewes' milk, 400 kilos at a time, this yoghurt is thick and creamy, and so sweet you don't need the honey and walnuts offered with it.

Stani, which opened in 1931 in Piraeus, has occupied the same tiny premises off Omonia Square since 1949. Like so much of the centre, its street is a mixed bag, combining ruined buildings with busy eateries, a gleaming neoclassical hotel and a tawdry cinema 'strictly for adults'.

But Stani's immaculate interior returns you to yesteryear with its period photos along with a framed award from the 1953 Thessaloniki International Fair. Interestingly, the founder of Stani – which means sheepfold – came from the same mountainous area beyond Delphi as the founders of Greece's two largest yoghurt companies, Delta and Fage, but the Karageorgos family has never wished to expand.

Indeed, the current owner, Thanasis, won't even sell his yoghurts to any other shop, much less open more. He takes pride in being small but genuine. 'Think of it,' he says, 'each yoghurt we make contains a trace of the original bacillus my grandfather used 90 years ago. Because we always keep back some to make the next batch. It's a natural, three-way unbroken chain since we also buy our milk from the same producer he did, and some of our old customers bring in their grandkids.'

In this changing city, Stanti remains 'a constant archive of tastes'.

**Address** Marikas Kotopouli 10, Omonia, Athens 10432, +30 210 5233637, www.stani1931.gr | **Getting there** Metro to Omonia (M2 & M3), and a two-minute walk | **Hours** Daily, early till late. Closed three days per year. | **Tip** Marika Kotopouli (1887–1954) was a famous stage actress who founded the Omonia Theatre later named after her (now the Rex), but she was also noted for her scandalous love affairs, some with younger actresses, as rumour had it.

# 96__Syngrou Forest

*An unlikely wilderness in a tycoon's estate*

This enormous (95 ha) tract of mostly unbuilt woods separates the municipalities of Maroussi and Kifissia and owes its existence to a remarkable woman, Iphigenia Syngrou. When her husband, Andreas, bought it around 1875, he was the most powerful man in Greece after King George I. A skilled but often unscrupulous banker, his name was linked to scandals and bankruptcies, tarnishing his reputation as financier and politician, but as a philanthropist he was unsurpassed. His donations built schools, hospitals and museums, funded disaster relief and continued after his death.

His wife Iphigenia encouraged him and was a philanthropist in her own right, especially concerned with children. But they also led a glittering social life in their palatial country house on the estate. With its crenellated roof, it looks anything but Greek. Equally anomalous is the ochre Gothic chapel next to it, the only Orthodox church with a steeple in Greece. Both were designed by Ernst Ziller, the most popular architect of the day.

When Syngrou died, he left it all to Iphigenia, but upon her death in 1920, she willed it to the Hellenic Agricultural Society (now the Institute of Agricultural Science), on condition that the land be used 'for the education of good farmers and gardeners'. This has kept the estate out of the clutches of would-be developers and while it does have some athletic facilities, beekeeping and planted areas, you can lose yourself in a natural pine forest. Only the distant traffic noise betrays the presence of the city.

The Institute conducts seminars and maintains a beekeeping museum and a cactus collection, but most visitors just use the vast unplanned space to walk their dogs, jog, bike, and look for birds, flowers and foxes on the asphalt or meandering dirt paths. The Friends of Syngrou volunteers clean up regularly, and mount a fire watch in summer. And the greenery makes Kifissia much cooler than the centre.

Address Between Maroussi and Kifissia, Kifissias 182, Maroussi 15124, +30 210 8011146 | Getting there Bus 550, A 7 or B 7; three entrances on Kifissias Avenue | Hours Sunrise to sunset. Institute not open to the public. | Tip The Anavryta school on the estate was built in 1949 at the instigation of Queen Frederica to educate crown prince Constantine. Then an élite private boarding school, along the lines of Gordonstoun, it went the way of the monarchy and is now a state lycée.

# 97 The Tactual Museum

*Getting a feel for antiquity*

Athens is renowned for its museums, packed with splendid finds gathered from a rich historical palimpsest, yet as with all museums in the world, the policy is to 'look, but don't touch'. There is one museum, however, where you will see visitors using their bare hands to explore every curve, line, corner, bump and fold of the historical exhibits.

The Tactual Museum, run by the Lighthouse for the Blind of Greece organisation, welcomes visually impaired as well as seeing individuals to feel plaster-cast masterpieces such as statues, wall reliefs, amphorae, theatrical masks, figurines and many other exact replicas of Greek antiquities from the Cycladic, Minoan, Geometric, Doric, Classical, Hellenistic and Roman periods.

Located in a two-storey neoclassical building, the spacious museum opened in 1984 and is home to the most noteworthy artefacts exhibited around the country and the world. The Venus de Milo, the Charioteer of Delphi, Hermes of Praxiteles, Poseidon of Artemision and the Archaic Kouros of Volomandra are just some of the exhibits you can connect with through your fingertips, all of them consistently maintained by archaeologists because they get worn from touch. On the ground floor you can get acquainted with Byzantine icons, marble slabs and an intricately carved wooden iconostasis.

The visually impaired and the sighted (the latter wearing a blindfold) are given an extensive tour by a volunteer guide to connect with the aesthetic form of the exhibits in ways that would be impossible simply through the power of visual observation. Sighted visitors may first take a look, but later, when blindfolded, they are encouraged to guess what they are touching with their hands. Regardless of whether you guess correctly or not, the sensation can be as disconcerting as when you feel lost, or exhilarating, when you experience art in such a novel way.

Address Doiranis 198, Kallithea 17673, +30 210 9415222, www.tactualmuseum.gr | Getting there Metro to Kallithea (M1), then bus 911 to Faros Tyflon | Hours Mon–Fri 9am–2pm | Tip Nearby, you'll find the Stavros Niarchos Cultural Centre where the National Opera and National Library are housed. You can roam the grounds, with its immense lawn, water features and Mediterranean garden, which forms a green roof over the Opera House and Library, breathe in the sea air and even rent a bike.

# 98 The Temple of the King

*A monument to Greece's greatest love – and rivalry*

When Panathinaikos is playing at home, the area around the old stadium is awash in green, the team's colour, and vibrates with an intense energy that reaches a crescendo with the exclamation 'gooooal!' In Greece, football is held above politics; team devotion may even come before God and country which, local loyalties notwithstanding, is divided between the two rivals at the top of the football pantheon – Panathinaikos and Olympiakos.

Greece, as Dionysis Savvopoulos sang, sighs in its football fields. In Panathinaikos' case, those sighs of heartbreak and happiness are captured within the walls of Apostolos Nikolaidis Stadium, the oldest in-use football arena. True fans never refer to the stadium by its official name; it's simply *I Leoforos* ('the avenue', from its address) and is hallowed ground. The club grew out of the neighbourhood and was, indeed, founded in 1908 in a home at Arahovis 40 in Exarchia. Its fame today is international but its roots are so firmly planted in the Ambelokipi, Neapoli, Pangrati and Patissia districts that the offer of a new stadium at a different site caused a fan rebellion. (Instead, management had to settle for basic renovations.) During construction in the 1920s, workers clashed with the refugees settling the neighbourhood who sought temporary shelter under its stands.

If football is the king of sports, to its fans Panathinaikos is the king of kings. Everyone has their own special memories from the *Leoforos* but a defining moment was the club's 8-2 rout of Olympiakos in 1930 and, of course, the season that ended with Panathinaikos in the 1971 European Cup final at Wembley Stadium. You can pick up memorabilia at the club's store on the Tsoha Street side, but don't be surprised by the prevalence of the number '13': it's a reference to Gate 13, the stadium section associated with the team's most dedicated (and loud!) fans.

**Address** Leoforos Alexandras 160, Ambelokipi 11634, +30 210 6444401, 210 8709000 | **Getting there** Metro to Ambelokipi (M3) | **Hours** Only on game days – check website www.pao.gr | **Tip** Restoration work at the Prosfigika, or refugee housing, across Alexandras is planned to preserve both the architecture and the bullet holes from civil war clashes.

# 99__To 24oro

*A greasy spoon for a city that parties all night*

Before you dive into the Athens clubbing scene, you need to stake out the all-night eateries where you can stave off the late-night munchies or soothe your stomach before hitting the pillow. Traditionally, revellers would head to the central meat market, mingling with the night workers just coming off their shifts. But as nightclubs moved from the centre to the southern coast, clubbers turned to 'To 24oro', literally the 24-hour place. Taxi drivers were first to discover it and no doubt helped spread the word to many of their late-night fares. Thus, in the space of three-plus decades since it opened, To 24oro has become a fixture on the Athens clubbing map.

Bleary-eyed revellers stumble in near dawn seeking the traditional Greek remedy after an alcohol-fuelled night on the town: a steaming bowl of *patsas* – a bracing broth that visually at least isn't for the squeamish despite its reputed roots in ancient Sparta.

Fans swear that there's nothing like it to settle the stomach after a long night, but a soup made from tripe and sometimes trotters can be unsettling for some. So even though *patsas* is the mainstay of its after-hours menu, To 24oro has stretched its offerings to other soups, fast food staples like pizza and burgers, late-night favourites like pasta and omelettes, and even barbecue to appeal to a clientele that has also expanded from after-hours to all hours. This includes the more recent addition of 'home-style' stews or *mageirefta*, the traditional Greek comfort foods.

The food isn't gourmet and it's certainly not good – in the health and nutrition sense, that is. But as late-night greasy grub goes, it's tops. The ambience is just what you'd expect from a fast-food-and-taverna combo, with short-order cooks who flip hamburgers, toss pizzas and grill chops at superhuman speeds that keep queues moving even on the busiest nights. Indeed, on those occasions, getting a table or ordering your food is less of a problem than finding a place to park or stop outside.

Address Leoforos Syngrou 44, Athens 11742, +30 210 9221159 | Getting there Metro to Syngrou-Fix (M 2); bus 1, 5, 10, 15, 40, 230, 550, A 2 or A 3 | Hours Open 24 hours | Tip Sample Greek rock or contemporary music at Stavros tou Notou (Tharypou 37), one of the city's top live venues.

# 100_To Kompoloi tis Psyrri
*All about worry beads, a unique Greek tradition*

Not long ago a man twirling worry beads was a common sight – on the street, in a café, on the train. Today, the smart phone seems to have taken their place. But Vasso Mahaira, owner of this beguiling shop, assures us that they will never go out of fashion.

'There's not a home in Greece that doesn't possess at least one set of beads. And they are one tradition that is exclusively ours. In other parts of the world, beads are associated with prayer and religion, but here they are used solely in order to relax, to relieve stress, for luck.'

According to Mrs Mahaira, prayer beads originated in India when an initiate made a string of 108 seeds to remind his teacher of the order of his prayers. The custom spread to the Muslims, who cut the number to 33, and to the Catholics with their rosaries. Although some say that a monk on Mount Athos introduced prayer beads to the Orthodox, Mahaira maintains that they weren't seen in Greece until the Ottomans took over and that Greeks copied the habit from the Turks, but lengthened the string to give them room to play. Greek beads have no fixed number but it must be odd, and a multiple of four plus one, strung on silk closed by a larger bead curiously called a papas or priest, with or without a tassel.

The shop's collection contains hundreds of beads, ranging from plastic for €5 to expensive creations made of amber, ebony, coral, wood, bone, antler, ivory, resin, apricot stones and more. They represent the passion of Vasso's late husband, Elias Saridakis, who from a child was entranced by the sight and sound of cool street guys whirling them in Psyrri.

Choosing worry beads is like selecting a crystal: feel them, play, rub them, smell them, listen to the music of the beads. Pick the natural material that speaks to you aesthetically and emotionally. Its positive energy could reduce your own addiction to your smart phone.

**Address** Agion Anargyron 13, Plateia Psyrri, Athens 10553, +30 210 3243012, www.kobojewels.gr | **Getting there** Metro to Monastiraki (M1 & M3), and a 10-minute walk | **Hours** Daily 10am–flexible, 7–11pm; closed only for Easter and Christmas | **Tip** Around the corner from the square, Karaiskaki is a unique street hung with dozens of different kinds of lamps.

# 101 To Koulouri tou Psyrri Bakery

*Sesame rings, the bread of memories*

'To Koulouri tou Psyrri' logos emblazoned on the trunks of scooters whiz round the city taking stacks of fresh-baked bread rings to street-corner vendors. They are a contemporary twist to the familiar sight of the *koulouri* seller pushing his cart through the streets. But mechanising delivery to street-corner *koulouri* sellers is the bakery's only update to the enduringly popular snack it began making in the 1960s.

The *koulouri*, of course, is much older than this unassuming enterprise in the heart of Psyrri. Dating back to the Byzantine Empire, the sesame-encrusted bread ring was originally associated with the cities of Constantinople and Thessaloniki. The association with Thessaloniki is still strong across Greece, except in Athens where local preference is for a thinner, crisper *koulouri*. But the technique is the same and the secret is in the starter, or *prozymi*, and wood-burning oven that draws out the nutty sweetness of the sesame seeds pressed into the surface.

The mark of a good *koulouri* is its aroma – not just while in the oven but hours later. Baking starts long before dawn, infusing the dewy morning air with the smell of freshly baked bread. Still warm, the rings are stacked, loosely packed, and despatched to selling points around Athens. Through the 1980s, it comprised the customary Greek breakfast for office workers and snack for school kids, eaten with a foil-wrapped wedge of processed cheese. Today it's often eaten plain, ever-popular even as the city bursts with shops selling far fancier baked goods.

A *koulouri* keeps well in a bag or backpack, a satisfying and nutritious energy boost on a day of sightseeing. Vendors are on many city centre streets or you can stop by the bakery in Psyrri. No need to ask directions: just follow your nose.

**Address** Karaiskaki 23, Psyrri, Athens 10554, +30 210 3215962 | **Getting there** Metro to Monastiraki (M1 & M3) | **Hours** Daily 7am–1pm | **Tip** Reward yourself for snacking healthily: pick up reworked vintage jewellery or other gifts at the Kartousa Gallery (Taki 9).

# 102　To Pagkaki

*A café with a philosophy, starting with no bosses*

At first glance, To Pagkaki (The Bench) looks like any of the other cafés on this pedestrian street. Funky, atmospheric hangouts and restaurants can be found on both sides, their chairs and tables inviting you to stop and enjoy the park-like trees and bushes planted all down the middle.

But To Pagkaki is different. It is an urban workers' collective, organised horizontally, with no hierarchy. All members get the same hourly wage regardless of their job, all decisions are taken jointly, and even their website switches from male to female pronouns to show recognition of gender equality. The idea was born in 2008 and the fact that they opened two years later, as the 'crisis' began, is pure coincidence.

Unemployed and anticapitalist, the original members wanted 'to provide a collective answer to the problems of daily life that would be useful to others instead of surrendering to depression and hopelessness'. They support small producers in Greece and like-minded groups abroad, buying their coffee from Zapatistas in Mexico and their sugar from the landless peasant movement in Brazil, avoiding named brands and supermarkets.

Their aim: to be affordable, encourage entertainment and creativity, share ideas and dreams, promote causes – like freedom for the Kurds, another egalitarian society – and donate profits where needed.

The place is casual and inviting, with mismatched tables and chairs, green and yellow walls (one hung with its emblem, a bicycle), a 'reading corner / library', and low music, from the public domain and Creative Commons 'because we don't like intellectual property'. A pot of tea comes with a bowl of thick honey, not a throwaway plastic container. And the surprisingly large menu is so tempting, the prices may call for a splurge. Quality is part of their philosophy too.

But don't go when there's a general strike. To Pagkaki will be closed in sympathy.

**Address** Georgiou Olimpiou 17–19, Koukaki, Athens 11741, +30 213 0009927, www.pagkaki.org | **Getting there** Metro to Syngrou-Fix (M 2) and a 10-minute walk; trolley 1, 5 or 15 to Koukaki, trolley 10 and bus 040, B 2, 126, 134, 136 or 137 to Olympiaki | **Hours** Daily 11–2am, Thu 3pm–2am | **Tip** The National Museum of Contemporary Art housed in the stunningly remodelled former Fix Brewery is just 10 minutes' walk from the café.

# 103__To Valsamo
### *The smallest shop in Athens*

Valsamo is a soothing herb (St John's wort in English), which has given us the word 'balm', as it's a panacea for almost every ailment. First touted by Hippocrates, *Hypericum perforatum*'s yellow flowers turn into a fragrant reddish lotion / tonic when soaked in olive oil in the summer sun. Good for the skin, aches and pains, internal, skeletal and muscular, a teaspoonful is said to even keep depression at bay.

The sight of this shop near the Central Market should chase off any blues. No bigger than a double wardrobe, it occupies a corner of Evripidou Street, the city's spice and herb souk, which boasts at least seven more, a decorative and aromatic nod to Greece's Anatolian heritage. There, garlands of peppers and branches of oregano dangle outside while other seasonings are scooped from open sacks.

At Athinas 40, To Valsamo stocks the same variety, all neatly packaged in see-through envelopes, tidily stacked on shelves that look too crammed to hold one more. There could be as many as 200 types, Greek and foreign, with the least in demand highest.

At Athinas 42, next to the market, a larger shop bears the same name, a newer, expanded version of the wardrobe / cupboard. Yannis Zervos, whose grandfather opened the first in the early '80s, mans the till there and is as knowledgeable as any pharmacist about the merits of each herb. His 'pappou' managed to set up the store only after many adventures: he left Lesvos alone at aged 10 in 1940, survived the war somehow, never went to school and worked in cafés and grocery shops before buying his own place.

A closer look reveals some mysterious translations: *taraxako* (dandelion) = shit, *apsithia* = unclean, *kritikos* = hungry. Yannis' father wrote the labels and he hasn't had time to correct them.

The biggest mystery is how Vassilis, who tends the kiosk, manages to stuff everything back inside at day's end.

Address Athinas 40, Athens 10551, +30 210 3250956, www.to-valsamo.gr | Getting there Metro to Monastiraki (M1 & M3) or Omonia (M1 & M2), and a 10-minute walk | Hours Mon–Sat 7am–5pm | Tip The Varvarkeios Market next door dates from 1886. For food lovers, it's a must, but the faint-hearted may be put off by dangling carcasses, pig and cow heads, buckets of innards and a certain reek. It conceals the Epirus taverna, a favourite with shoppers and market workers.

# 104 Tournavitou Street

*A bright spot in the 'neighbourhood of the undistinguished'*

With house numbers ending at 13, Tournavitou might not be the shortest street in Athens, but it is certainly the most rainbow hued. Each of its low buildings is painted a different colour, from sky blue to fire-engine red, butter yellow, pistachio green and even Cycladic white.

The street encapsulates the latter-day history of Psyrri. Forty years ago, this neighbourhood of low houses adjoining Monastiraki and the market district was the domain of professions that no longer exist – carters, spring makers, wood and charcoal sellers – as well as bourgeois families. Because of its proximity to the ancient cemetery, it was known as 'stachtothiki' (ash container). But by the late '90s, nightclubs, restaurants, bars and even a theatre had replaced the dying businesses and Tournavitou became 'hot'.

Alas, with Greece's slump, most of these closed too and the semi-abandoned street became derelict. When appeals for help to local authorities went unheard, Themis Vasarmidis, owner of the last surviving club, Tin Pan Alley, resolved to change this image. He commissioned well-known street artist, Achilles, to paint a double mural on one half-destroyed façade; area residents helped transform the buildings; and Laniz, an iconographer, created a stylised gold tree with a trio of birds in its branches against the pistachio-green wall.

Today, even Tin Pan Alley is shut except for special events, but the Theatro Thission stages performances all winter for both children and adults. And at the top end of the street wooden chairs, a few tables and a collection of bric-à-brac signal the precarious existence of one of the area's few remaining traditional shops, Athanasopoulos Karekladiko, chair repairs.

As Yannis Athanasopoulos said, 'Everyone does what they can to keep Tournavitou cheerful, and Tin Pan Alley keeps its walls graffiti free with repeated coats of paint.'

Address Tournavitou, Psyrri, Athens 10553 | Getting there Metro to Thissio (M 1), and a five-minute walk | Tip You can see more of Achilles' street art outside the Imanta vinyl shop opposite the chairs and in a parking lot for the Psyrri cinema off Sarri, one street away.

# 105 Underground Nazi Prison

*Kommandantur jail cells a 'Space of Remembrance'*

Every step down takes you further from the expansiveness and light of Korai Square into the darkness of a basement some six or seven metres beneath the street. This is more than a metaphoric descent into hell: for the thousands of Greeks brought here by the Nazi *Kommandantur* it was a trip to Hades. Reaching the first level, you're still on familiar 'museum' turf; one level down, the emptiness is so overwhelming that you can't breathe. You begin to feel what it was like being a prisoner here.

Soon after the Nazi troops seized Athens in April 1941, the *Kommandantur* took control of the building – an architectural gem redesigned for the National Insurance Company in the mid-1930s that had been commandeered for the civil service at the outbreak of World War II. The basement had a bomb shelter – cramped, dark, airless and perfect for the *Kommandantur* to use as detention cells for suspected resistance members. Men, women, even children, grabbed in raids or neighbourhood sweeps, were brought here, questioned, tortured and then sent either to jail, concentration camps or execution. The terror experienced by some of these captives is still palpable in the scrawled messages on the walls: a name, an age, a profession, 'I want water', how they ended up here, random drawings, a heart.

Today, the building bustles with life, in the office suites above and the cafés crowded into the impressive marble lobby. A cinema occupies much of the basement but a small area has been preserved as it was when the *Kommandantur* used it for its interrogations. The only change is the Nazi flag hanging on one wall and that once adorned the Gestapo headquarters nearby. Rather than brightening the room, the splash of colour is like a large spattering of blood – a vivid reminder of the war years.

Address Korai 4, Athens 10564, +30 210 3243581 | Getting there Metro to Panepistimio (M 2); bus 2, 3, 4, 5, 11, 25, 26, 27, 54, 220, 221, 230, 608, 622 or 790 | Hours Tue – Sat 9am – 2pm | Tip The Gestapo headquarters was less than a kilometre away, in Kolonaki (Merlin 6). The site is marked by an old door and a bronze and metal relief depicting an anonymous resistance fighter.

# 106__Varsos

*Athens' oldest sweetshop-café, preserved in amber*

The first Varsos brothers opened shop in central Athens in 1892 and moved to their present premises in Kifissia 30 years later – 'when the floor collapsed'. It hasn't had a facelift since the mid-1960s. Walk past the tables in front and you enter a vast chamber lined by giant refrigerators, display cases and marble counters cluttered with jams, nuts, pastries, sugary biscuits, savoury pies, a bowl of strained yogurt, tarts and cakes, custards, jellies and towers of empty boxes stamped with the red and blue Varsos logo.

Apart from a few vintage photos and an early price list, no attempt has been made to give the place a snazzy look, but the heady aroma of newly baked goods lures you in. Stroll to the seating area at the rear, and you'll ogle shelves of *tsourekia* (brioches), an infinity of meringues, and hundreds of different types of sweets, biscuits and confections.

Not even the owners, the grandsons and great-grandsons of the founders, can tell you how many products are on offer, but they know without benefit of a computer database exactly when something will run out. The most famous of these – yoghurts, pies, rice puddings, *tsourekia*, mille-feuilles – are made daily from fresh eggs (500 to 1,000), milk (300 to 700 litres), butter, plus sugar and flour, using no preservatives. 'Just like we did in the old days.'

Coming from the mountains of central Greece, the original Varsos lads sold only milk, yoghurt and cheese, but branched out into milk-based desserts and more sophisticated sweets under the influence of the cooks in Kifissia, a district of grand mansions where rich Athenians spent their summers.

The big café area is neither welcoming nor charming, and sometimes its clientele look as fossilised as the shop, but the nostalgia factor is sufficient to draw in scores of families and 40-somethings who long for the tastes and atmosphere of their childhood.

**Address** Kassavetes 5, Kifissia 14562, +30 210 8012472, 210 8013743, www.varsos.gr |
**Getting there** Metro to Kifissia (M1), then a five-minute walk; two minutes from A7
and 550 bus terminus on Kifissias Avenue | **Hours** Mon–Fri 7–1am, Sat 7–2am,
Sun 7am–midnight | **Tip** On the corner of Kifissias and Kassavetes stop to look at four
sarcophagi 'in a glass cage', relics of the Roman era and a piece of Roman retaining wall.

# 107_ The Vespasianae

*Where the phrase 'to spend a penny' was first used*

At the north-east corner of the Roman Agora or Wheat Bazaar, as the Greeks called it, look to your right and you'll see the outline of a rectangular building with a marble floor. A closer look will reveal a raised bench with two holes in it. These are all that remain of the 68 seats in what used to be a very important facility in the busy commercial market, the public latrines.

The walled 16-by-18-metre structure had an entrance lobby and an atrium over the square sitting area for ventilation and light. It also possessed continuous running water that flowed in a channel around the room and then into a drain connected to the city sewers. The toilets offered seclusion from passers-by but hardly privacy as we know it, because the seats were only 56 centimetres apart.

Non-existent until the Romans took over Athens, public loos were *de rigueur* in every one of their cities, and one cannot overemphasise their importance to civilisation! The emperor Vespasian, however, is credited with introducing them in 74 A.D. and then taxing their use to boost the state coffers, which were empty after a disastrous civil war. It is he who said 'pecunia non olet' (money doesn't stink) when his fastidious son Titus objected to the 'urine tax'. Vespasian is alleged to have waved a coin under Titus' nose, asking whether he detected an odour. Receiving a negative answer, he revealed its origins.

But one must remember that, because of its ammonia and mineral content, urine played an important role in the tanning industry, as a whitener in laundry, and even in mouthwash and toothpaste, a practice that continued until the 17th century. Once taxed, it wasn't wasted.

Today in Italy and in Greece, outdoor public toilets are called Vespasianae, but the name didn't come into use until the 19th century. Among the emperor's other projects funded by the money they raised was the Colosseum.

Address Roman Agora, Polignotou 3, Monastiraki 10555, +30 210 3243220 | Getting there Metro to Monastiraki (M1 & M3), and a five-minute walk | Hours Mon–Fri 8am–3pm, Sat & Sun 8am–5pm | Tip The largest structure in the Agora is the Fethiye or Mosque of the Conquest, built by the Ottomans to commemorate either their conquest of Crete in 1686–1688 or their reconquest of Athens after the Venetians' brief occupation during which Morosini (in)famously bombed the Parthenon.

# 108_ Vorres Museum

*Greek culture summarised in a unique rural home*

What does a 3,000-year-old marble washtub have in common with a 19th-century porcelain plate, a Byzantine icon, a peasant rug, a rustic chair or a 20th-century abstract painting? Answer: they are all emblematic of Greek civilisation, whether the work of a modern master or an anonymous, ageless craftsman. And they were all irresistible to journalist Ion Vorres, when he returned to his birthplace in 1962 after spending 18 years in Canada.

What he found distressed him. The post-war recovery was destructive and unplanned. Apartment blocks sprouted where traditional homes had stood and mod cons took the place of antiques and antiquities. Vorres resolved to save what he could and chose Paiania, an almost abandoned village at the foot of Mount Hymettus, for his refuge.

He had no intention of creating a museum; he just wished to preserve the best of the past, the folk culture that combined utility with elegant design. Watching him buy three houses and six acres of land, connect and furnish them with humble and priceless finds, his neighbours thought he was mad. Then his interest turned to modern Greek art, which he collected with the same passion and taste.

Vorres died in 2015, but he has left an incomparable homage to Greece, harmoniously blending past and contemporary with nature. A white patio opposite the entrance holds sculpture, but much of the modern art collection – with paintings representative of every big name in Greece – lies discreetly underground. A secret door at the end leads to a 200-year-old room, linking the 20th century to a different era and then to a courtyard, bounded by beautiful drystone walls and adorned with trees, flowers and ancient or traditional objects, like well heads or Ali Baba jugs. The complex of rooms and courtyards, gardens and galleries, forms a unique oasis, a repository of the best of Greece. Every detail fits.

**Address** Parodos Diadochos Konstantinou 1, Paiania 19002, +30 210 6642520, 210 6644771, www.vorresmuseum.gr | **Getting there** Metro to Nomismatokopio (M3), then bus 125 or 308 to Paiania, get off at Agia Triada, and then a five-minute walk; or metro to Doukissis Plakentias (M3) and bus 307 to Paiania, Agia Triada | **Hours** Sat & Sun 10am–2pm; weekdays by appointment | **Tip** Paiania was the birthplace of Demosthenes, the stammerer who became the world's greatest orator.

# 109__The VR Project
## *Going virtually anywhere in Athens*

On any swelteringly hot summer (or blustery winter) day in the Greek capital one can be teleported from a cacophonous Monastiraki street to the icily crisp, pristine silence of Mount Everest, a shipwreck with a whale for company at the bottom of the ocean, a sunny but comfortably cool ancient Greek temple or even to the dusty surface of the moon alongside Neil Armstrong aboard the Apollo 11. All that without the heatstroke and ensuing delirium that comes with it. How? By visiting the polished, ultra-modern world of The VR Project, just a few minutes' walk from boisterous Monastiraki Square. With some of the most sophisticated virtual reality technology on the global market today (HCT Vive Headsets), this is an escape few locals and tourists visiting Athens are yet to be acquainted with.

Some regulars come to the minimalist space, renovated from an old industrial unit above a souvlaki shop, with its glass rooms and giant screens after a day drenched in mundanity to find other-worldly peace; immersed in the deep blue surrounded by glow-fish, creating life-size 3D paintings that include glittering stars and rainbows that they can stand within, raising their adrenaline by shooting intergalactic weapons at monsters best left behind in the virtual world, or deactivating time bombs.

Also designing their own apps via the VR Project Lab, the owners of The VR Project, Yiannis Parcharidis and Loukas Katsikaris, collaborate with archaeologists to teleport visitors to archaeological sites such as the Temple of Poseidon at Cape Sounion, where unlike being there in the flesh, you can stand inside and observe the details in the ancient columns and participate in digs. Soon it will be possible to travel to classical sites in the multicoloured glory of their original state to experience what they were like at the time. So real you can almost touch the stones.

Address Athinas 18, Monastiraki 10551, +30 210 3821832, www.thevrproject.gr | Getting there Metro to Monastiraki (M1 & M3), then a five-minute walk | Hours Tue–Fri 4–10pm, Sat 2–11pm | Tip Just two streets down from Athinas, at a distance of around five minutes' walk on Agias Theklas Street you'll find Melissinos, The Poet Sandal Maker, famous for his tailor-made classical Greece-inspired footwear that has been worn by The Beatles, Jackie Onassis and Elizabeth Taylor.

# 110 Vryssaki with a View

*A creative hub and picturesque café at once*

Many who visit laid-back, village-like Vryssaki café-bar's rooftop to drink up views of romantic Plaka's ceramic-tiled rooftops, the Acropolis and the Stoa of Attalos, are quite unaware that they're sitting in what's also a dynamic multi-arts space. The place is the vision of solicitor George Neris, who actually grew up in a house next door to Vryssaki (until the 1970s the shared-home premises of several provincial families).

It all began when he set up Synthesis, the company that kicked off the Athens Fringe Festival in 2012. Seeing hundreds of new artists participating to showcase their work, Neris soon realised that what he was organising in a month could run throughout the year and include far more variety. His principle was to reject the conventional top-down approach and go horizontal instead, so he turned Vryssaki into a café and multi-space where individuals were encouraged to create their own small, self-governed communities. Over the past eight years, the place has become a thriving platform for educational, artistic and sociopolitical initiatives. Programmes range from a popular Solidarity training workshop, gastronomy courses, art exhibitions and academic or cultural talks to dance or theatre performances, children's activities and creative labs.

Neris, who has successfully implemented similar programmes in London via ArtFix UK, keeps wanting 'to offer a suggestion of how things can develop in the future, in a world where work flexibility is increasingly important'. He suggests visitors go to Vryssaki to chat to people around them and exchange ideas, to discover new perspectives and ways of helping each other, to stop by the help desk and learn what (often free) events are taking place, and how you can execute your own short-term or long-term projects. Or you can just stick to Greek coffee and a relaxed chat in the scenic, familial ambience.

Address Vryssakiou 17, Plaka, Athens 10555, +30 210 3210179, www.artfix.gr | Getting there Metro to Monastiraki (M1 & M3); bus 025, 026, 027, 035 or 227 | Hours Daily 11am–10pm | Tip A few streets down is The Elytis House, where you can see photos, furniture and the study where the national poet Odysseas Elytis created his Nobel Prize-winning works.

# 111 Yannis Pappas Studio

*The private man behind the public monuments*

The phrase 'Greek sculpture' conjures up images of battle scenes, gods and mortals with such perfectly chiselled detail that the chiton does seem to be gossamer rather than marble. Greeks' love of statuary has remained steadfast through the millennia, with public parks and buildings liberally accented with sculptures even though both creations and creators draw far less admiration and hardly any attention. Chief among them is Yannis Papppas (born 1913), whose work graces buildings around Greece or stands outside them, but his name is barely known outside art circles.

Pappas, who died in 2005, has an impressive resumé. He studied at the École des Beaux-Arts and the School of Law in Paris concurrently, then spent time at the Louvre and Musée National des Monuments Français (cast museum) before returning to Greece. Over seven decades he produced over 700 works, and his busts alone could fill an exhibition. Many of his commissions were for figures and busts of politicians but also other artists such as Yannis Moralis. Perusing these is like flipping through the pages of modern Greek history – Makrygiannis, Korais, Odysseas Elytis, and a fascinating series of Eleftherios Venizelos forms.

All this is pleasantly displayed in his former studio, a two-storey stone and wood porticoed villa, which his son donated to the Benaki Museum to match the artist's bequest of his works. A neighbouring lot was purchased to expand the garden, creating a visual breech in this suburb's tightly packed apartment blocks. Paintings, sketches and more abstract sculptures illustrate the range of the artist's talent and perhaps true aesthetic as they radically depart from the style of his public sculptures. It's especially interesting to note the influence of Egyptian monumental art in his work from his war service there.

Best of all, this isn't a museum but a working studio used by the students of the Athens School of Fine Arts.

Address Anakreontos 38, Zografou, Athens 15772, +30 210 3671000 | Getting there Bus 235 or 608 | Hours Tue, Fri & Sun 10am–2pm | Tip A horse named Argentinos at the Maroussi Riding Club (Paradisou 18) was used as the model for the statue of Alexander the Great, which took the artist 32 years to complete.

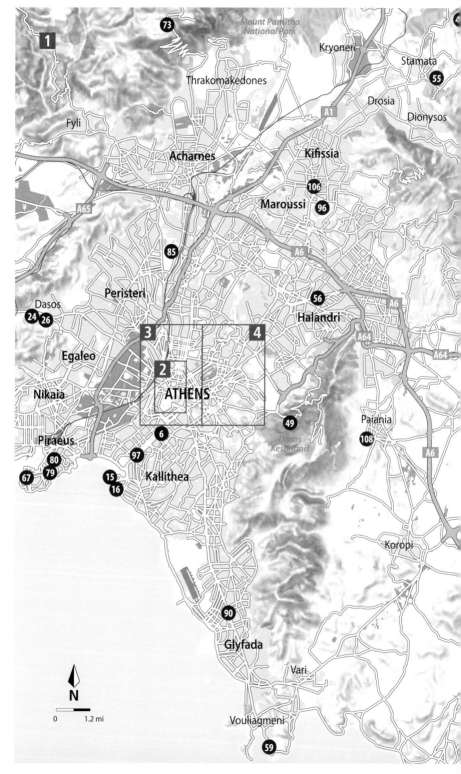

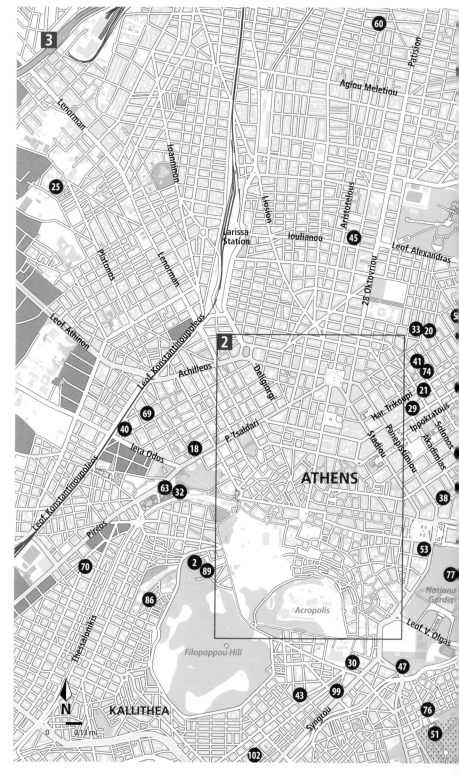

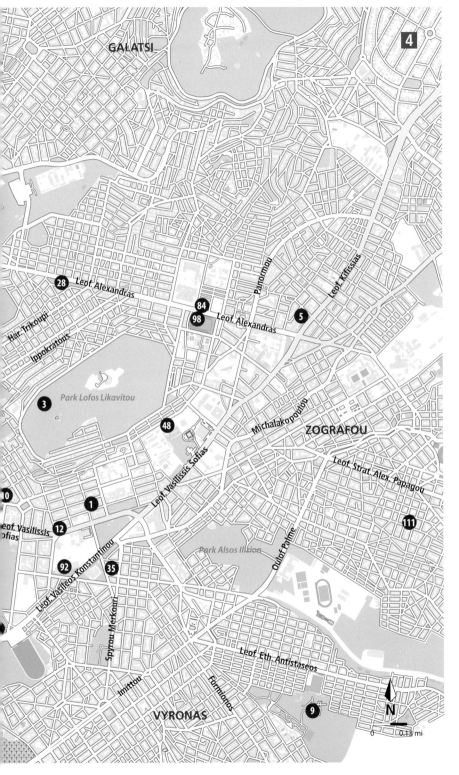

Peter Eickhoff
**111 Places in Vienna**
**That You Shouldn't Miss**
ISBN 978-3-95451-206-5

John Sykes, Birgit Weber
**111 Places in London**
**That You Shouldn't Miss**
ISBN 978-3-95451-346-8

Rüdiger Liedtke
**111 Places on Mallorca**
**That You Shouldn't Miss**
ISBN 978-3-95451-281-2

Dirk Engelhardt
**111 Places in Barcelona**
**That You Must Not Miss**
ISBN 978-3-95451-353-6

Annett Klingner
**111 Places in Rome**
**That You Must Not Miss**
ISBN 978-3-95451-469-4

Marcus X. Schmid
**111 Places in Istanbul**
**That You Must Not Miss**
ISBN 978-3-95451-423-6

Christiane Bröcker,
Babette Schröder
**111 Places in Stockholm**
**That You Must Not Miss**
ISBN 978-3-95451-459-5

Giulia Castelli Gattinara,
Mario Verin
**111 Places in Milan**
**That You Must Not Miss**
ISBN 978-3-95451-331-4

Laszlo Trankovits,
Rüdiger Liedtke
**111 Places in Cape Town**
**That You Must Not Miss**
ISBN 978-3-95451-610-0

Jo-Anne Elikann
**111 Places in New York**
**That You Must Not Miss**
ISBN 978-3-95451-052-8

Frank McNally
**111 Places In Dublin**
**That You Must Not Miss**
ISBN 978-3-95451-649-0

Matěj Černý, Marie Peřinová
**111 Places in Prague**
**That You Shouldn't Miss**
ISBN 978-3-7408-0144-1

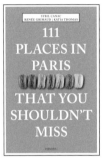

Sybil Canac, Renée Grimaud,
Katia Thomas
**111 Places in Paris**
**That You Shouldn't Miss**
ISBN 978-3-7408-0159-5

Thomas Fuchs
**111 Places in Amsterdam**
**That You Shouldn't Miss**
ISBN 978-3-7408-0023-9

Kai Oidtmann
**111 Places in Iceland**
**That You Shouldn't Miss**
ISBN 978-3-7408-0030-7

Kay Walter, Rüdiger Liedtke
**111 Places in Brussels**
**That You Shouldn't Miss**
ISBN 978-3-7408-0259-2

Andrea Livnat,
Angelika Baumgartner
**111 Places in Tel Aviv**
**That You Shouldn't Miss**
ISBN 978-3-7408-0263-9

Tom Shields, Gillian Tait
**111 Places Glasgow**
**That You Shouldn't Miss**
ISBN 978-3-7408-0256-1

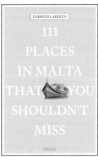

Fabrizio Ardito
**111 Places in Malta**
**That You Shouldn't Miss**
ISBN 978-3-7408-0261-5

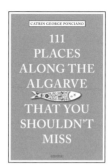

Catrin George Ponciano
**111 Places along the Algarve**
**That You Shouldn't Miss**
ISBN 978-3-7408-0381-0

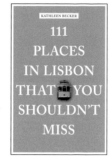

Kathleen Becker
**111 Places in Lisbon**
**That You Shouldn't Miss**
ISBN 978-3-7408-0383-4

Alexandra Loske
**111 Places In Brighton**
**And Lewes That You**
**Shouldn't Miss**
ISBN 978-3-7408-0255-4

Gillian Tait
**111 Places in Edinburgh**
**That You Shouldn't Miss**
ISBN 978-3-95451-883-8

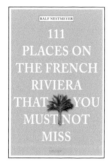

Ralf Nestmeyer
**111 Places on the**
**French Riviera**
**That You Must Not Miss**
ISBN 978-3-95451-612-4

Ralf Nestmeyer
**111 Places in Provence**
**That You Must Not Miss**
ISBN 978-3-95451-422-9

Lucia Jay von Seldeneck,
Carolin Huder
**111 Places in Berlin**
**That You Shouldn't Miss**
ISBN 978-3-95451-208-9

Stefan Spath
**111 Places in Salzburg**
**That You Shouldn't Miss**
ISBN 978-3-95451-230-0

*Acknowledgements*

Many friends have made suggestions that helped us in our selection
of these 111 places, and we're especially grateful to the following:
Isabella Curtis, Aristotelis Dimitsas, Giorgos Giorgopoulos, Vasilis
Haralambidis, Nota Hatzopoulou, Brady Kiesling, Anne Kokotos,
Petros Ladas, Eleni Marneri, Mina Mitsobonou, George Neris,
Vivienne Nilan, Foivos Oikonomides, Rosie Randolph, Silvi Rigo-
poulou, Alexander Seferiades, Christa Vayannos and Sarah Yu.

*The photographer*

**Yannis Varouhakis** was born in Athens in 1979
and has been a professional photographer since
2001. He has collaborated with different magazines and newspapers
like *Kathimerini*, *Gynaika*, *Pontiki* and others, shooting portraits and
landscapes in Greece and abroad. He has also worked around the
theatre and the arts, photographing dance, concerts, movie produc-
tions and shows.

*The authors*

For over 20 years **Alexia Amvrazi** has been writing about Greece for global media and copywrites for branding companies. She's been a regular contributor to *The Wall Street Journal Europe* and Greecetravel.com and is currently running the popular wellness website imverywellthankyou.com. Writing aside, for a decade she presented a daily show on national radio, does voiceover work and video reporting.

**Diana Farr Louis** has lived in Athens since 1972. Her travel writings include guidebooks, *Secrets of the Greek Islands, Athens and Beyond* and *Travels in Northern Greece*. Besides numerous articles on food for Greek and international publications, she is the author of cookbooks on the Ionian Islands and Crete, co-editor of *A Taste of Greece*, and a regular contributor to www.culinarybackstreets.com

**Diane Shugart** is author of *Athens by Neighborhood* and was editor of *Odyssey*, a US-based magazine about Greece. She writes widely on Greek politics and culture, served as consulting editor for several guidebooks, and translates academic non-fiction. Having recently completed a post-graduate course on antiquities trafficking, she is researching a book on cultural heritage and civil war.